Life of Fred® *Dogs*

Stanley F. Schmidt, Ph.D.

Polka Dot Publishing

ISBN: 978-0-9791072-7-6

Library of Congress Catalog Number: 2011924328
Printed and bound in the United States of America

Polka Dot Publishing   Reno, Nevada

To order copies of books in the Life of Fred series,

visit our website PolkaDotPublishing.com

Questions or comments? Email the author at lifeoffred@yahoo.com

Eighth Printing

Life of Fred: Dogs was illustrated by the author with additional clip art furnished under license
from Nova Development Corporation, which holds the copyright to that art.

for Goodness' sake

or as J.S. Bach—who was
never noted for his plain
English—often expressed it:

Ad Majorem Dei Gloriam
(to the greater glory of God)

If you happen to spot an error that the author, the publisher, and the printer missed, please let us know with an email to: lifeoffred@yahoo.com

As a reward, we'll email back to you a list of all the corrections that readers have reported.

A Note Before We Begin the Fourth Book in the Series

The secret is out. Fred is not a Super Hero.

He can't fly. He doesn't even own a cape.

He has no super powers. He can't see through walls.

Not Fred

He is not big, strong, or handsome.

He is a grossly underpaid ($500/month) teacher at a poorly run university somewhere in Kansas. He teaches from 8 to 5 every day with a five-minute break at 3.

He has no guile. He is not crafty. Evil men, such as C. C. Coalback, find it easy to take advantage of him.

Fred makes mistakes, but he doesn't get angry.
His doll, Kingie, can draw much better than he can, but he doesn't have envy or resentment.

When people mistreat him, he doesn't seek revenge.

In Sunday School, Fred had been told that Mr. Micah (6:8) wrote that God only requires three things: act justly, love tenderly, and walk humbly. Fred tries to do that.

He has a *joie de vivre*, a delight in being alive. In the previous book, Fred broke into singing songs of happiness that he had made up. They weren't very good songs, and he sang them off-key with his squeaky five-year-old voice.

In short, Fred looks like a failure in everything—except in those things that really count.

LEARNING MATHEMATICS

Whether there is joy in learning mathematics depends so much on how it is taught.

In the first four chapters of this book, you will see a master teacher at work with his students. He presents $8 + 8 = 16$ in a way that causes his students to break out in applause. Fred puts a lot of work into presenting $8 + 8 = 16$, and his students will remember it for a lifetime.

THREE TYPES OF MATH BOOKS

Almost every math book for pre-college kids falls into one of three categories. Open up a book to somewhere in the middle and start reading. In half a minute, you can tell which category it is in.

Category #1: Drill and Kill

A procedure is presented. The page is decorated with some politically correct picture, and the child has 30 boring problems to do. The problems look like they were produced by a robot and are designed to beat the concept into the child's head.

$$\begin{array}{ccccccccc} 8 & 8 & 8 & 8 & 8 & 8 & 8 & 8 & 8 \\ +8 & +8 & +8 & +8 & +8 & +8 & +8 & +8 & +8 \end{array}$$

Here is the procedure. Here are the problems. The students are rarely given a reason to learn the procedure. Learning math becomes just a part of the pain of being a child.

Category #1: Drill and Kill is the most common math curriculum.

Category #2: Fluff and Giggles

Lots of color. Reading these books is like eating cotton candy. Every page is sunshine. The temperature is always 72°. Get out your crayon and write in the book. No brain strain.

okay everybody! Which one has wheels?

Category #3: Fred

Who would want a book that is:
* ☆ fun to read
* ☆ complete*
* ☆ inexpensive
* ☆ motivating**

daughter Jill, age 3 months

I do!

HOW THIS BOOK IS ORGANIZED

Each chapter is about six pages. At the end of each chapter is a Your Turn to Play.

Have a paper and pencil handy before you sit down to read.

Each Your Turn to Play consists of some interesting questions. Have your child write out the answers—not just orally answer them.

After all the questions are answered, take a peek at my answers that are given on the next page. At this point your child has *earned* the right to go on to the next chapter.

Don't allow your child to read the questions and just look at the answers. Your child won't learn as much taking that shortcut.

---

* I know of no other math curriculum that contains more mathematics than the Life of Fred series.

** Every part of mathematics comes from the everyday life of Fred. There is a concrete reason for learning it. It is not just "for college."

Contents

Chapter One
A Million Jobs

Fred loved to teach. And he had the perfect job: he was a teacher. It was a couple of minutes before his first class of the day was scheduled to begin.

He walked into the Archimedes Building, down the hallway, and into his giant classroom. Hundreds of students were sitting in their seats, taking out their pencils and paper, and getting ready to listen to Fred.

In the years that he had been teaching at KITTENS University, the sight of his students coming into his classroom always excited him. He was like an actor getting ready to go on stage.

❀ ❀ ❀

There are a million (1,000,000) different jobs to choose among.

Fred could have been a bus driver, except they don't let a five-year-old get a driver's license.

 He could have been a brick layer, except that he was too short. And five-year-old boys have not yet developed muscles to carry a lot of bricks.

Being a bullfighter was out of the question. Fred would not have enjoyed killing (or being killed).

There are people who make perfect bus drivers, brick layers, or bullfighters. Fred wasn't one of them.

We each have a place in the Dance of Life in which to do our dancing. Some will be mothers, some will be moose trainers, and some will be mushroom farmers. Fred is a teacher.

It was eight o'clock. The students became quiet and waited for Fred to begin.

Over the years, Fred had won many awards for his teaching. Students loved attending his classes. He made it fun.

Fred dashed into a back room and put on a chef's hat.

He pushed a large stove out to the front of the class.

It moved easily. It was on rollers.

Joe and Darlene were two students in the class. Darlene liked to sit next to Joe.

Joe said, "Look! He's bringing out a stove."

Darlene had already noticed that and so had everyone else in the classroom.

Joe had been the last one to notice it. He had been drawing on his paper.

He liked to draw dinosaurs.

Arithmetic class

Tuesday, February

Bow wow

for lunch
    cookies
    Sluice
    candy

Darlene told Joe it was time to pay attention.

Joe wrote on his paper: ⏱ 2 💰 a 10 shun

Fred climbed up a ladder to the top of the stove and began frying eggs.

Joe wrote 4 in his notes.

Fred took a second pan and fried some more eggs.

Joe wrote 2 Darlene crossed it out and wrote 3.

"Now," said Fred, "if I flip the three eggs in the second pan into the first pan, what do I get?"

Joe raised his hand and shouted out, "An omelette!" He smiled and looked at Darlene. He was sure that he had given the right answer.

Fred wrote on the blackboard:

$$\begin{array}{r} 4 \\ + \ 3 \\ \hline 7 \end{array}$$

Please take out a piece of paper and write your answers before checking your work on the next page. Please.

Some of these questions are from things you studied in the previous Life of Fred books.

Your Turn to Play

1. There are maybe a million different jobs that adults do. Write down a list of three jobs that you would *not* be interested in doing. Be creative. Don't use any of the jobs mentioned already in this chapter.

2. Copy these on a piece of paper and answer them:

$$\begin{array}{ccccc} 4 & 7 & 5 & 0 & 9 \\ + \ 9 & + \ 4 & + \ 6 & + \ 3 & + \ 1 \\ \end{array}$$

3. 4 eggs + 3 eggs = 7 eggs.

   4 mice + 3 mice = ?

   $4x + 3x$ = ?

   $4\pi + 3\pi$ = ?

   π is a Greek letter.

4. What is the cardinal number associated with the set {Darlene, Joe}?

·······ANSWERS·······

1. Your answers may be different than mine. Here are some jobs that I, myself, would not like to do:

✓ parachute tester (I don't want to jump out of a plane.)

✓ pyramid salesman

✓ piano mover

2.
$$
\begin{array}{ccccc}
4 & 7 & 5 & 0 & 9 \\
+\,9 & +\,4 & +\,6 & +\,3 & +\,1 \\
\hline
13 & 11 & 11 & 3 & 10
\end{array}
$$

3. 4 mice + 3 mice = 7 mice

$4x + 3x = 7x$

$4\pi + 3\pi = 7\pi$

4. The cardinal number of a set is the number of members the set has. The cardinality of {Darlene, Joe} is 2.

Chapter Two
Doubles

Fred gave the fried eggs to some of the students who hadn't had breakfast that morning.

"Today," Fred announced, "we are going to play a game called Doubles."

He pointed to the back two burners on the stove and said, "Two." He pointed to the front two burners and said, "Two."

"How many burners are on the stove?"

Joe carefully counted the burners and held up four fingers.

Fred wrote on the board:

$$\begin{array}{r} 2 \\ +\ 2 \\ \hline 4 \end{array}$$

Fred began to wash the pans. He poured three ounces of soapy water into each pan and asked, "How many is three plus three?"

He wrote on the board:

$$\begin{array}{r} 3 \\ +\ 3 \\ \hline 6 \end{array}$$

Darlene wrote in her notes:

Two 2s are 4.

Two 3s are 6.

Fred finished washing the pans. He used four cupfuls of clean water to rinse out each pan.

Fred wrote on the board:
$$\begin{array}{r} 4 \\ +\ 4 \\ \hline 8 \end{array}$$

Fred held up his two wet hands and said, "Five fingers on each hand."
$$\begin{array}{r} 5 \\ +\ 5 \\ \hline 10 \end{array}$$

Darlene wrote in her notes:

Two 2s are 4.

Two 3s are 6.

Two 4s are 8.

Two 5s are 10.

Fred turned off the lights in the classroom.

Joe said to Darlene, "Oh, we get to see movies. I like that."

Joe took out some popcorn that he always carried with him. He couldn't watch a movie without eating popcorn.

Fred showed a picture of the egg carton that he had taken before he had removed the seven (3 + 4) eggs to cook them.

Actual Photograph

Fred said, "There are six eggs in each row. Six plus six equals a dozen."

$$\begin{array}{r} 6 \\ +\ 6 \\ \hline 12 \end{array}$$

Joe turned to Darlene and asked, "Whenf as der mofkey gonga ztarf?"

Darlene told him, "Don't talk with your mouth full. It's not polite."

In a couple of minutes, he was able to chew and swallow all the handfuls of popcorn he had stuffed into his mouth. He repeated his question, "When is the movie going to start?"

"There isn't going to be a movie," Darlene explained. "Fred just showed us a picture of a dozen eggs so that we could learn that six and six make a dozen."

"Oh," said Joe. "Why didn't he say that?"

"He did. You weren't listening."

Joe wrote down what he had just learned . . .

which was nothing.

Fred had to work harder to illustrate the bigger doubles.

7	8	9	10
+ 7	+ 8	+ 9	+ 10
14	16	18	20

To illustrate that 7 + 7 = 14, Fred showed pictures that his doll Kingie had drawn of the seven days of the week.

Fred began, "Everyone knows that there are seven days in a week."

Then he asked, "Does anyone know how long a fortnight is?"

The class was quiet.

Fred continued, "*Fortnight* is from the Middle English word *fourtennight* which came from the Old English words *feowertene niht*."

The class was still quiet.

"A fortnight is 14 days and nights—two weeks. Here is a fortnight."

Your Turn to Play

1. Fred started to write this chart on the board. Finish it up to 10 + 10.

   •   1 + 1 = 2

  ••   2 + 2 = 4

 •••   3 + 3 = 6

2. 14 is a number. It has two digits: 1 and 4.
A thousand is a number. It has 4 digits: 1, 0, 0, and 0.
How many digits are in the number one million?

3. < means *less than*. Which of these are true:

   5 < 8   100 < 1,000   44 < 6   0 < 1

. . . . ANSWERS . . . .

1.

• •	$1 + 1 = 2$
•• ••	$2 + 2 = 4$
••• •••	$3 + 3 = 6$
•••• ••••	$4 + 4 = 8$
••••• •••••	$5 + 5 = 10$
•••••• ••••••	$6 + 6 = 12$
••••••• •••••••	$7 + 7 = 14$
•••••••• ••••••••	$8 + 8 = 16$
••••••••• •••••••••	$9 + 9 = 18$
•••••••••• ••••••••••	$10 + 10 = 20$

> *Did you notice . . .*
> When you double a number, the answer is always even.

2. One million (1,000,000) has 7 digits.

3. $5 < 8$ $100 < 1{,}000$ $44 < 6$ $0 < 1$
     true   true   false   true

Chapter Three
Mickey Was Unavailable

A fortnight was the perfect way to illustrate that 7 + 7 = 14. A carton of eggs was a great way to remember that 6 + 6 = 12.

Fingers come in fives.

It takes four cupfuls of water to rinse a pan.

But Fred was baffled,
>befuddled,
>>perplexed, and
>>>puzzled how to show that
>>>8 + 8 = 16.

What comes in eights? he thought to himself.

He had once seen a man riding a ladybug that had eight spots on its right side. If there were eight spots on its left side, that would show that 8 + 8 = 16.

He knew 10 + 10 = 20 would be pretty easy.
Two dimes equal 20 cents.

How can I show 8 + 8 = 16? Fred wondered.

Time Out!
A call to Disneyland

Then he thought of a second way to show that 8 + 8 = 16, since it was pretty hard to find a man riding a ladybug.

He remembered that cartoon characters are often drawn with four fingers on each hand.

If Fred could get someone like Mickey Mouse and his girlfriend to come to his classroom, all his students would remember forever that 8 + 8 = 16.

He telephoned Disneyland and asked to speak with Mr. Mouse.

He was told that Mickey wouldn't be able to make it to Fred's classroom this February.

Fred knew what to do. He ran back to his office and got his doll Kingie. They headed into the room behind his classroom where he kept all his costumes and makeup. They put on special gloves with only four fingers on each hand.

When Fred and Kingie appeared, all the students clapped. The students would never forget 8 + 8 = 16.

Joe turned to Darlene and said, "Look! It's Mickey!" Joe was completely fooled by Fred's and Kingie's disguises.

Darlene's notes were very neat:

Two 2s are 4.

Two 3s are 6.

Two 4s are 8.

Two 5s are 10.

Two 6s are 12.

Two 7s are 14.

Two 8s are 16.

Joe wrote down what he had just learned . . .

which was nothing.

Arithmetic class
Tuesday, February

dozen
Mickey came to class!!!!

Bow wow

for lunch
cookies
Sluice
candy

Fred and Kingie headed into the room behind the classroom.   They took off their ears and gloves. Kingie decided to wait in that room until Fred was finished teaching for the day. Kingie wasn't very good at walking and liked to be carried by Fred.

When Fred came back into the classroom, Joe turned to Darlene and said, "It's too bad Fred wasn't here to see Mickey."

Joe raised his hand and asked, "You said that *fortnight* is a word from used English." Sometimes Joe's questions sounded more like statements than questions.

Hidden inside his statement was, "Would you please explain that?"

Fred responded, "I said that *fortnight* is from the Middle English word *fourtennight* which came from the Old English words *feowertene niht*. Old English is not the same as used English."

Fred needed to do a little more explaining: "English is not the same as math. When your great-great-great grandmother added together two apples and two apples, she got four apples. That math doesn't change.

"In contrast, English is constantly changing in all kinds of ways. First of all, new words are constantly being added. In the 1940s, we added words like *baby-sit, bikini*, and *quiz show*. In the 1950s: *do-it-yourself, parenting*, and *fast-food*. In the 1960s: *bumper sticker, fortune cookie*, and *hippie*. In the 1970s: *couch potato, hot tub*, and *sunblock*. In the 1980s: *buffalo wing, decaf*, and *high-five*. In the 1990s: *bad hair day, latte*, and *mouse potato*."

Your Turn to Play

1. Somewhere between 1990 and 1995 the phrase *mouse potato* came into the English language. Can you guess what it means?

2. Authors have to be very careful to match the language in their novel to the time in which the story is set. Suppose you were writing a World War II (1939–1945) novel: `The captain walked into the mess hall and ordered a hamburger and a latte.  He set his assault rifle on the table and brainstormed with his buddies about how to get more soldiers interested in the aerobics program.` Would any words need correcting?

3. Copy these on a piece of paper and answer them:

$$
\begin{array}{ccccc}
6 & 4 & 5 & 0 & 23 \\
+\,7 & +\,7 & +\,6 & +\,9 & +\,1 \\
\end{array}
$$

4. What number added to itself equals 16? In algebra, we let x be an unknown number. $x + x = 16$.

. . . . ANSWERS . . . .

1. *Mouse potato* was patterned after *couch potato,* which is a person who spends too much time in front of a television set.

For *mouse potato,* substitute *computer* for *television.*

2. *Latte* isn't the only anachronism.*

Assault rifle came into the English language in the 1970s.

Brainstorming came into the English language in the 1950s.

Aerobics came into the English language in the 1960s.

Mess hall is fine. It entered the English language in the 1860s.

3.

6	4	5	0	23
+ 7	+ 7	+ 6	+ 9	+ 1
13	11	11	9	24

4. What number makes $x + x = 16$ true? If we let x equal 8, we get $8 + 8 = 16$, which is true.

 Did cavemen know about Fred?

---

* *Anachronism* (a-NACK-reh-NIS-em) A goof in assigning something to the wrong time. Soldiers in the Civil War (1861–1865) did not have BandAids® or Kleenex®.

Chapter Four
English Has Changed

Fred continued explaining to Joe about how English has changed over the years. It wasn't just the fact that new words are added to the language.

In addition to changes in vocabulary, English has had changes in pronunciation and in grammar over the years.

Here is the official chart.

> 450–1100 Old English (the poem *Beowulf*)
> 1100–1500 Middle English (*The Canterbury Tales* by Chaucer)
> 1500–1650 Early Modern English (Shakespeare, King James Bible)
> 1650–now Modern English

GO BACK ABOUT 400 YEARS

to Early Modern English, and you may need some help with some of the vocabulary of Shakespeare and the King James Bible.

GO BACK ABOUT 600 YEARS

to the Middle English of *The Canterbury Tales*:

And Palmeres for to seeken straunge strondes,
To ferne halwes, kouthe in sondry londes.*

---

* And pilgrims seek foreign shores to distant shrines that are consecrated in sundry lands.

GO BACK ABOUT 1000 YEARS

to the Old English of *Beowulf:*

Hwæt! Wé Gárdena in géardagum

þéodcyninga þrym gefrúnon

hú ðá æþelingas ellen fremedon.*

We don't use the letters þ or ð anymore. Nowadays you will still see æ: "Give Cæsar what belongs to Cæsar. . . ." (James Moffatt's 1928 translation of part of Matthew 22:21.)

Joe was amazed. He didn't know that English had changed so much.

Just last week, Joe was at a factory and saw a funny machine. He asked what it was and someone told him it was a time clock. Joe misunderstood and thought it was a Time Machine.

Joe had always loved stories of King Arthur and the Knights of the Round Table. With this Time Machine, Joe dreamed of going back to visit

---

* Listen up! We—of Danes-carrying-spears and their kings in days of long ago—have heard of their brave fighting.

King Arthur and Guinevere and all the Knights of the Round Table and have some pizza.*

The Round Table was first mentioned in literature in 1155, so if Joe used his Time Machine and went back about 900 years, he wouldn't understand what they were saying.

Fred wrote on the board numbers that add to 13:

$$\begin{array}{ccccc} 4 & 5 & 6 & 7 & 8 \\ +9 & +8 & +7 & +6 & +5 \\ \hline 13 & 13 & 13 & 13 & 13 \end{array}$$

and told his students that <u>these</u> <u>will</u> <u>not</u> <u>change</u>. A thousand years from now eight plus five will still be thirteen.

English changes.

Astronomy changes. In 2006, Pluto was no longer a planet.

Biology changes. A lot of examples are given in *Life of Fred: Pre-Algebra 1 with Biology.*

Computers change. In the old days, they couldn't beat everyone on the planet in chess.

But in math, eight plus five equaled thirteen when *Beowulf* was written, and eight plus five equals thirteen today.

———————————————

* Joe was mixed up.

Fred still had one puzzle to solve. He had shown a way to remember 5 + 5 = 10 using the fingers of both hands. He had shown how to remember 6 + 6 = 12 with a picture of two rows of eggs.

A fortnight was the way to remember that 7 + 7 = 14.

When he and Kingie pretended they were cartoon characters with four fingers on each hand, he showed that 8 + 8 = 16.

Two dimes are 20¢ showed 10 + 10 = 20.

But how to show 9 + 9 = 18? He asked the class if anyone could think of anything in ordinary life where nine plus nine equaled eighteen.

The class was quiet. Well . . . almost everyone was quiet. Joe had gotten hungry and even though it wasn't nine o'clock yet, he decided to start eating his lunch.

Crunch! Crunch! Crunch! Joe liked dry spaghetti for lunch. He would pull out a piece of spaghetti and chew on it. The noise drove Darlene nuts.

As everyone was looking at Joe eating his dry spaghetti, Fred had an idea. He walked over to Joe.

Joe thought Fred wanted some of his spaghetti to eat.* He offered Fred the box.

Fred took out **(Guess how many!)** sticks of spaghetti, showed them to the whole class, broke them in half, and handed the 18 pieces back to Joe.

Your Turn to Play

1. Joe was delighted. He turned to Darlene and said, "I gave Fred 9 sticks, and he gave me 18. I now have more spaghetti."

Darlene shook her head. She couldn't believe Joe thought he had more spaghetti after Fred had broken the nine pieces in half.

She took out a single stick and told Joe, "Watch me make you a whole lot of spaghetti!" She broke it in half. Then took the two pieces and broke them.

1→2→4→8→16→ . . .

Continue this series.

2. Find a value of x that makes x + x = 14 true.

3. Find a value of y that makes 6 + y = 8 true.

4. Find a value of z that makes 7 − z = 4 true.

---

* This is silly. Everyone knows that, as a general rule, there are two times when Fred does not eat: (1) when he is in a classroom, and (2) when he is not in a classroom.

. . . . ANSWERS . . . .

1.

1→2→4→8→16→32→64→128→256→512→1,024→2,048
→4,096→8,192→16,384→32,768→65,536→131,072

→262,144→524,288→1,048,576→2,097,152→4,194,304

→8,388,608→16,777,216→33,554,432→67,108,864→134,217,728

→268,435,456→536,870,912→1,073,741,824→2,147,483,648→4,294,967,296

→8,589,934,592→17,179,869,184→34,359,738,368→68,719,476,736→137,438,953,472

→274,877,906,944→549,755,813,888→1,099,511,627,776→2,199,023,255,552→4,398,046,511,104

→8,796,093,022,208→17,592,186,044,416→35,184,372,088,832→70,368,744,177,664

→140,737,488,355,328→281,474,976,710,656→562,949,953,421,312→1,125,899,906,842,624

→2,251,799,813,685,248→4,503,599,627,370,496→9,007,199,254,740,992 By this time, Darlene had broken and doubled the stick of spaghetti 53 times.

After 70 "doubles" she had 1,180,591,620,717,411,303,424 sticks.

After a hundred "doubles" she had: 1,267,650,600,228,229,401,496,703,205,376 sticks. One nonillion, two hundred sixty-seven octillion, six hundred fifty septillion, six hundred sextillion, two hundred twenty-eight quintillion, two hundred twenty-nine quadrillion, four hundred one trillion, four hundred ninety-six billion, seven hundred three million, two hundred five thousand, three hundred seventy-six. Each of these sticks was very small.

2. x + x = 14 will be true when x is 7.

3. 6 + y = 8 will be true when y is 2.

4. 7 − z = 4 will be true when z is 3.

Chapter Five
Three Messengers

It was ten minutes to nine. (Or 8:50, if you prefer.) In ten minutes, Fred's eight o'clock arithmetic class would be over.

He handed each student A Row of Practice. This was a teaching aid that Fred had invented. It gave the students some practice doing addition but didn't take an hour to do.

He held up an example so that everyone could see. He told them, "Cover

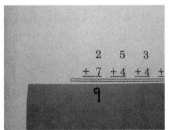

the gray answers with a blank sheet of paper. Write your answers on your paper. After you have done the whole row, check your answers."

$$
\begin{array}{rrrrrrrr}
6 & 9 & 5 & 4 & 5 & 8 & 8 & 22 \\
+5 & -2 & +8 & +9 & +2 & +1 & +3 & +1 \\
\hline
11 & 7 & 13 & 13 & 7 & 9 & 11 & 23 \\
\end{array}
$$

Joe wasn't paying attention when Fred gave the instructions. When he got his paper, he turned to Darlene and said, "Look. All the answers are right there."

He traced over the gray answers to make them darker . . . and learned nothing.

The students who had memorized their addition facts finished A Row of Practice in less than a minute.

Just then, a special messenger came into the classroom and handed Fred:

KITTENS University

Special Bulletin

To all faculty, students, and staff:

Hi. Today is Tuesday. I thought it would be nice for us all to meet in my office at 9 a.m. today. I want to talk about what we are going to do on Valentine's Day.

Our University President Speaks

Then a second messenger came in and gave Fred this memo:

> Memo to all faculty, students, and staff:
> From:
>
>   My secretary just told me that all of the faculty, students, and staff won't fit in my office.
>   Let's cancel the 9 o'clock classes and meet in our football stadium.

Fred couldn't believe this. Yesterday, the university president had canceled all the classes because of the bad weather. Today, there will be no classes at 9 a.m. because he wants to talk about Valentine's Day.

Fred had the silly idea that the most important thing a university should be doing is educating its students.[*]

As Fred began to read this second notice to his students, a third messenger came in and gave Fred this scrap of paper:

> Hi again everyone. My secretary just told me that it is too cold to meet in the football stadium. Classes are canceled for the rest of the day. Your President

---

[*] Is that such a silly idea?

That meant that Fred had to cancel his

Beginning Algebra class,
Advanced Algebra class,
Geometry class,
Trigonometry class,
Calculus class,
Statistics class,
Linear Algebra class, and
Seminar in Biology, Economics, Physics, Set Theory, Topology, and Metamathematics.

That's a lot of education that wasn't going to happen.

Darlene handed Joe the one nonillion, two hundred sixty-seven octillion, six hundred fifty septillion, six hundred sextillion, two hundred twenty-eight quintillion, two hundred twenty-nine quadrillion, four hundred one trillion, four hundred ninety-six billion, seven hundred three million, two hundred five thousand, three hundred seventy-six spaghetti sticks, and he put them back into his box of spaghetti. Joe popped 11 jelly beans into his mouth and in one giant bite, he turned them into 22. 11 + 11 = 22.

$$\begin{array}{r} 11 \\ + \ 11 \\ \hline 22 \end{array}$$

He then suggested, "Hey. Since we don't have any more classes today, why don't we go out and eat?"

Darlene thought to herself: *Eat! You've been eating for the last hour. It is only nine o'clock. How could you be hungry?* What she said was, "Sure. That would be great. I'm not very hungry right now, but you could eat for both of us."

Joe smiled. He thought Darlene enjoyed watching him eat. She just liked being with him.

Choices	CHOICES	Choices
Choices	*Choices*	CHOICES

small essay

Making Choices

Everyone makes choices.

When Fred was very young, he chose to read a lot of books. That was a good choice for him. It allowed him to become a teacher at KITTENS University.

Joe chooses to eat all the time, even when he is not hungry. By the time he is 40, he will have a big belly and climbing stairs will begin to get difficult.

Some choices are lightweight. Waffles or pancakes? Does it make much difference? Which kind of sunglasses? Does it really matter?

Some people practice being cheerful.

Others choose to practice being a grouch.

It is a choice. Who do you think will have more friends?

You have many choices in life. How happy you will be depends on those choices.

You have a choice:

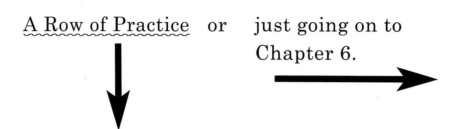

A Row of Practice   or   just going on to
Chapter 6.

Cover the gray answers with a blank sheet of paper. Write your answers on
your paper. Then after you have done the whole row, check your answers.

$$
\begin{array}{cccccccc}
9 & 11 & 6 & 3 & 8 & 4 & 3 & 33 \\
+4 & -2 & +5 & +8 & +5 & +5 & +4 & +1 \\
\hline
13 & 9 & 11 & 11 & 13 & 9 & 7 & 34
\end{array}
$$

Many choices are between two alternatives:

The Easy Way	The Hard Way
Immediate pleasure followed by long-term grief.	Difficult now followed by happy years later.

◉ Eating lots of double-chocolate cookies.
   Years of being fat.
◉ Watching garbage on television.
   Years of ignorance.
◉ Racing motorcycles in the dark on icy roads.
   Years of being dead.

◻ Not venting your anger at your friend.
   Years of having a friend.
◻ Reading good books—not trashy novels.
   Years of knowing.
◻ Practicing the piano.
   Carnegie Hall.

Chapter Six
A Postcard

red was alone. The classroom was empty. The students had headed out to do the things they do on a day of vacation.

It was quiet. It was warm in the room. There was no class to teach at nine o'clock.

Fred always carried at least one book with him for times like this. Today he was carrying Daniel Defoe's *Robinson Crusoe*,* Mortimer J. Adler's *How to Read a Book*,** and the first volume of *The Feynman Lectures on Physics*.***

The chairs in the classroom were too big for Fred to sit in comfortably. He headed off to a corner of the room with his books.

Fred was alone. He picked up his *Robinson Crusoe* book—a story about a man who was alone on a tropical island. Fred imagined what

* This is the first book that I, your author, ever read. (Warning: There are no girls in this book. Boys tend to like this book more than girls do.)

** *How to Read a Book* is not about how to open a book and know that c-a-t spells cat. It is not about reading newspapers or stop signs or *Dizzy Duck Dines on Doughnuts*. It is guidelines for getting the most out of heavy reading—where the reader is intensively involved. It is about real education: it's about growing up.

*** *The Feynman Lectures* may not be the best place to start to learn physics. Fred had already read many other physics books.

it would be like. He would build a little hut out of palms. He would swim in the warm ocean.

He turned a page and out fell a piece of paper. This wasn't that unusual. Fred sometimes bought his books at the used book store on campus. Frequently people would leave things in the books they sold to the store.

Sometimes it was a little bookmark. Sometimes a bus transfer. Today it was a photograph of a sunset. *Oh, how pretty!* Fred thought to himself. It was a picture postcard.

Fred turned it over and read:

Dear C.C. Coalback,

I'll be flying in to see you on the first Tuesday in February. I just . ... -.-. .- .--. . -.. *from* .--. .-. .. ... --- -. and you can hide me.

Regards,

S. Snow

To:

C.C. Coalback

KITTENS

Kansas

This is the first Tuesday in February! Fred thought. *And a secret code! I wonder what those dots and dashes mean?*

Fred took out his Morse code card and started decoding the secret message.

I just . .... -.-. .- .--. . -.. *from* .--. .-. .. ... --- -. *and*
     e s c a p e d   p r i s o n
you can hide me.

A =	• —
B =	— • • •
C =	— • — •
D =	— • •
E =	•
F =	• • — •
G =	— — •
H =	• • • •
I =	• •
J =	• — — —
K =	— • —
L =	• — • •
M =	— —
N =	— •
O =	— — —
P =	• — — •
Q =	— — • —
R =	• — •
S =	• • •
T =	—
U =	• • —
V =	• • • —
W =	• — —
X =	— • • —
Y =	— • — —
Z =	— — • •

Fred stood up. At first, he didn't know what to do. He did know that five-year-olds do not capture guys who have escaped from prison.

Then he realized that catching escaped prisoners is something that the police do.

Catch crooks ➜ the police

Just like:

Fix a pipe leak ➜ a plumber

Fly a plane ➜ a pilot

Fix broken bones ➜ a doctor

Deliver letters ➜ a letter carrier

Take money at a grocery store ➜ a cashier

In math, this is an example of a **function**. *For each thing you tell me, I give you one answer.* If you said, "Drive a cab," I would say, "Cab driver." If you said, "Heal sick cats and dogs," I would say, "Veterinarian." If you said, "Prepare meals in nice restaurants," I would say, "Chef."

This function associates to each thing that needs to be done, a person that does it.

I could invent a function that associates to each number its double.

1 ➔ 2

2 ➔ 4

3 ➔ 6

4 ➔ 8 and so on. You tell me a number and I give you one answer.

I could invent a function that associates to each person, the number of hairs they now have on their head.

Darlene ➔ 142,605 hairs

Joe ➔ 98,322 hairs

Fred ➔ 0 hairs

Donald Duck ➔ 0 hairs (Ducks do not have hair.)

For a function, you say something and I give you *one* answer. When you say, "Joe," the number of hairs on his head *right now* is one number, not two different numbers.

It's fun to invent functions. One function could be to associate with each book the number of pages it has.

Life of Fred: Dogs ➜ 128 pages

Dizzy Duck Goes to the Dentist ➜ 16 pages

Stan's Favorite Pizzas ➜ 8,220 pages

Your Turn to Play

1. Guess what the rule is for this function:

    1 ➜ 3

    2 ➜ 4

    7 ➜ 9

    30 ➜ 32

    100 ➜ 102

    116 ➜ 118

    > What do you do to get from the number on the left of the arrow to its answer?

2. Here is a harder one to guess:

     ➜ 4

     ➜ 2

     ➜ 8

     ➜ 0

     ➜ 2

...... ANSWERS ....

1. For the function

$$1 \rightarrow 3$$
$$2 \rightarrow 4$$
$$7 \rightarrow 9$$
$$30 \rightarrow 32$$
$$100 \rightarrow 102$$
$$116 \rightarrow 118$$

whatever number you gave me, I added two to it.

2. The rule I was thinking of was, "You tell me what it is, and I will tell you how many legs it has."

The Function PARTY GAME

How to Play:

One person thinks of a function and gives lots of examples.

Everyone else tries to guess the function.

Example:
Roger ➔ No
Michelle ➔ Yes
Harry ➔ No
Doris ➔ Yes

Rule: Is it a girl?

Example:
Roger ➔ 0
Michelle ➔ 3
Harry ➔ 1
Doris ➔ 1

Rule: Number of rings they are wearing.

Example:
Cat ➔ 3
Dog ➔ 3
Snake ➔ 5
Bumblebee ➔ 9

Rule: Number of letters in the word.

Example:
Roger ➔ 8
Michelle ➔ 8
Harry ➔ 9
Doris ➔ 8

Rule: How old are they?

Chapter Seven
Police Station

It was a six-minute walk to the police station. The police station was the largest building on campus. It had gold doorknobs and a stainless steel roof.

Fred was afraid to approach the building. It looked so expen$ive. The building cost a billion dollars ($1,000,000,000) to build.

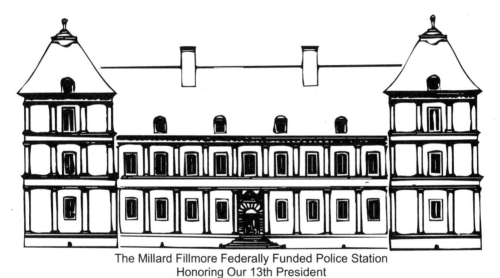

The Millard Fillmore Federally Funded Police Station
Honoring Our 13th President

But Fred knew that he had to report this escaped prisoner who was coming to KITTENS University to hide.

Fred held the postcard in one hand so that if anyone in the police station asked him why he was there, he could quickly show them the card.

He slowly opened the door. It was quiet inside. Fred tiptoed in. The floors were highly polished marble. The walls had patterns of inlaid stone.

Along one wall was

Fred saw the pattern. He knew that the next one would be a 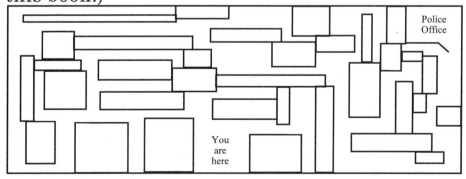 , since the pattern was

of the form <u>AAB</u> <u>AAB</u> <u>A</u>.

On another wall, he found the directory for the building. (Use your finger and show how Fred can get to the police office. Do not write in this book.)

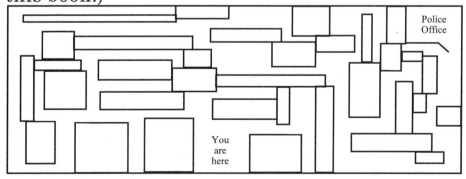

With postcard in hand, Fred entered the police office. A police officer was sitting at a desk. He looked at Fred and said, "Hi sonny. What can I do for you?"

Seeing that Fred had a card in his hand, he said, "Did you want a dog license for your dog?"

Fred shook his head. He was afraid to speak.

"Did you lose your dog? We can help you find it."

Fred shook his head again. He didn't want to be arrested for losing his dog.

Time Out!
Thinking clearly

Fred really wasn't thinking very clearly at this point. ① He hadn't eaten in several days. ② He was frightened by the giant building. ③ He had important news to tell the policeman.

If the policeman had asked Fred what $9 + 9$ was equal to, Fred might have forgotten that $9 + 9 = 18$.

Fred didn't realize that you can't be arrested for losing your dog.

And besides . . . Fred didn't own a dog.

Fred just held out his postcard. The policeman looked at the pretty picture and told Fred that he wasn't interested in buying postcards.

Fred turned the card over and handed it to him.

The policeman read it for a moment and said, "This is the first Tuesday in February. And Silvia Snow was an escaped prisoner. But we caught her a while ago and she's now back in prison."

The policeman pointed to the stamp on the card and told Fred that this card had probably been mailed years ago.

Fred gave the policeman a weak smile. He was embarrassed. He didn't know what to do. He turned around and headed out of the office and down the hall. The rubber soles on his jogging shoes squeaked on the polished marble floors.

Poor kid, the policeman thought to himself. *He didn't say a word. He must be very shy. He's probably the kind that would never be able to give a speech in public.*

Little did the policeman know that this was Professor Fred Gauss who lectures daily[*] for hours in front of large audiences.

Your Turn to Play

1. On the way out of the building Fred found another wall with a pattern on it.

What will the next image be: a swan or a moose?

2. Fred had memorized a lot of poetry. As he walked through the police station halls, he recited:

Tell men of high condition,	A
that manage the estate,	B
Their purpose is ambition,	A
Their practice only hate:	B
And if they once reply,	C
Then give them all the lie.	C

> *The Lie* by Sir Walter Raleigh, 1552–1618

Many poems rhyme. Condition rhymes with *ambition, estate* with *hate*, and *reply* with *lie*. The pattern of rhyming is called a rhyme scheme. In this poem, the rhyme scheme is ABABCC—the first and third lines rhyme; the second and fourth rhyme; the fifth and sixth rhyme.

What is the rhyme scheme for:

> *In Memoriam* by Tennyson, 1809–1892

Behold, we know not anything;
I can but trust that good shall fall
At least—far off–at last, to all,
And every winter change to spring.

---

[*] Except, of course, when the university president cancels classes.

·······ANSWERS·······

1.

has the pattern <u>AAAB</u> <u>AAAB</u> <u>AA</u> so the next thing will be an <u>A</u>, which is a .

The whole wall looked like: <u>AAAB</u> <u>AAAB</u> <u>AAAB</u> <u>AAAB</u> <u>AAAB</u> <u>AAAB</u> <u>AAAB</u> <u>AAAB</u> <u>AAAB</u> <u>AAAB</u> <u>AAAB</u>.

2. The rhyme scheme for:

Behold, we know not anything;	A
I can but trust that good shall fall	B
At least—far off–at last, to all,	B
And every winter change to spring.	A

is ABBA.

A later stanza in this poem reads:

So runs my dream: but what am I?
An infant crying in the night:
An infant crying for the light:
And with not language but a _____.

How would you end this line? His rhyme scheme is ABBA.

Pick one: And with not language but a bite.
And with not language but a cry.
And with not language but a diaper.

There are only two addition facts for numbers that add to 15:

$$6 \qquad 7$$
$$\underline{+\ 9} \qquad \underline{+\ 8}$$
$$15 \qquad 15$$

Please memorize these before you begin Chapter 8.

Chapter Eight
A Free Class

It was 10 o'clock when Fred emerged from the police station. For most people, when they step out into the bright sunlight from a dark building, it takes them a moment for their eyes to adjust to the light.

In a dark room, their pupils are large to let in a lot of light.

In the bright sunlight, their pupils contract.

For Fred, his eyes were always ready for the sunlight.  His eyes are always dots.

That's why you never see Fred with sunglasses.

Read all about it!

Fred purchased the latest edition of the campus newspaper.

THE KITTEN Caboodle

The Official Campus Newspaper of KITTENS University   Tuesday 10:00 a.m.   10¢

President Cancels Classes

KANSAS: An hour ago the president of KITTENS University canceled classes for the rest of the day.

President with His New Skis

A Caboodle reporter went to the president's office to investigate.

His secretary said that the president wasn't there. He had gone skiing.

Wow! Fred thought. *A free class in tumbling. I've never done that before.*

The address—789 Main Street—was easy to memorize. The three-digit number 789 had digits 7, 8, 9 that were consecutive numbers.

These are consecutive numbers: 55, 56, 57, 58, 59, 60, 61.

These are consecutive even numbers: 80, 82, 84, 86, 88, 90, 92.

These are consecutive odd numbers: 17, 19, 21, 23, 25, 27, 29, 31, 33.

Fred ran over to the new gym at 789 Main Street. He could hardly wait to take his free gym class.

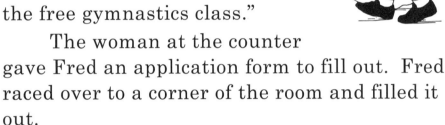

Fred rushed up to the front counter and said, "I'm here for the free gymnastics class."

The woman at the counter gave Fred an application form to fill out. Fred raced over to a corner of the room and filled it out.

Application Form

Name   Fred Gauss

Address   Room 314, Math Building, KITTENS

Bank   KITTENS Bank

Your PIN at the ATM of your bank   3141

Fred printed his answers very neatly. He wanted to make a good impression.

Time Out!
Personal Identification Number

PIN means Personal Identification Number. If you have someone's ATM card and their PIN, you can get money out of their bank account.

Because of that, you never should tell anyone your PIN.

Fred was way too trusting.

Fred handed the woman behind the counter his completed application form.

She said, "That will be one dollar please."

Fred was surprised. "I thought the class was going to be free."

She smiled and said, "Certainly, the class is free. This is just a small fee to cover the computer processing of your application."

Fred thought, *A dollar isn't that much, especially since they are giving me a free class.* He handed the woman a dollar.

She pointed to the men's locker room and said, "You can go in there to change."

Fred didn't know what to do. "I don't have any gymnastics clothes."

"That's okay. Most people do not. The man in the locker room will take care of you."

The man in the locker room looked at Fred and asked him where his father was. Fred didn't know since he had not seen his father in years. Fred shrugged his shoulders.

"Well," the locker room attendant said, "who's going to pay for your gym shirt rental?" He pointed to a sign on the wall.

Official
Gym Shirt
Rental

$1.00

"But I already have a shirt," Fred protested.

"That won't do," he was told. "Everyone in the class needs to wear a Coalback gym shirt. The class goes better if all the students are dressed alike."

It's only a dollar, Fred thought. *Besides, they are giving me a free class.* He handed the attendant a dollar and asked for an extra-extra small shirt.

Your Turn to Play

1. What is the smallest 4-digit number?

2. What is the largest 4-digit number?

3. Name two consecutive numbers so that the smaller is a one-digit number and the larger is a two-digit number.

4. Fill in the blank: When you count by twos—2, 4, 6, 8, 10, 12,—you are using consecutive _____ numbers.

```
........ANSWERS........
```

1. The smallest 4-digit number is 1,000.

2. The largest 4-digit number is 9,999.

3. Two consecutive numbers so that the smaller is a one-digit number and the larger is a two-digit number would be 9 and 10.

4. When you count by twos, you are using consecutive _even_ numbers.

A Row of Practice. Cover the gray answers with a blank sheet of paper. Write your answers on your paper. Then after you have done the whole row, check your answers.

8	7	5	7	6	7	3	38
+ 7	− 2	+ 2	+ 6	+ 9	+ 8	+ 6	+ 1
15	5	7	13	15	15	9	39

Chapter Nine
Just a Dollar

Fred stood there in the locker room. He had already spent a dollar for the application form and a dollar for the Coalback gym shirt rental.

"And gym pants?" the attendant asked as he pointed to another sign.

Fred shrugged his shoulders and thought, *That really isn't that much to rent official Coalback gym shorts, and besides, all of the people in the class will look alike and the class will go better.* He handed the attendant a dollar and got a pair of extra-extra small shorts.

And gym socks. Another dollar.

And gym shoes. Another dollar.

And a rental fee for the locker. Another dollar.

And a combination lock for the locker. Another dollar.

And the combination number for the combination lock. Another dollar.

And the shower fee. And the towel fee. And the bathroom sink fee (for the water and soap). And the bathroom mirror fee (in case you look in the mirror).

Fred held up his hand and said, "Excuse me. Why is there a fee for the bathroom mirror? I wouldn't think that looking in the mirror would wear out the mirror."

The locker room attendant explained, "We use that dollar to pay a man to keep the mirror clean. We wouldn't want our customers to have to look into a dirty mirror."

"Oh," said Fred. He handed over another dollar. "I think that's the last dollar I have with me. The rest of my money is in the bank."

"That's fine," said the attendant. "That's all the miscellaneous fees that we have. Remember that your class is free."

The attendant was lying. He had a long list of fees along with the excuses if anyone complained: warm air fee (it cost money to heat the building), shower drain fee (we have to pay a plumber if the drain gets clogged), carpet fee (we have to replace the carpet every year), locker room attendant fee (we have to pay him to help our customers in the locker room). . . .

The attendant was to charge these fees until the customer ran out of money. And each time he collected a dollar he was supposed to say, "And remember, the class is free."

Fred quickly changed into his official Coalback gym shirt. It was too big for him. He looked at the label on the shirt. It said, "One size fits all."

His official Coalback gym shorts and the socks and the shoes were all too large. Fred told himself, *They want everyone in the class to look alike so that the class will go better.*

He put his regular clothes in the locker and locked it with the lock he had rented. Fred thought, *I'm glad they rented me the combination lock. Now I know that my stuff is safe.*

The gym clothes were a bit too large for him. Note the x-ray view of his feet in the shoes.

The attendant pointed the way to the gym and gave Fred a little wave goodbye. Fred liked that.

The minute that Fred was gone, the attendant headed to Fred's locker and opened it. The gym had rented Fred the combination lock and the combination number, but the attendant had kept a copy of the number.

He threw the tiny shirt on the floor. And the tiny bow tie that Fred liked to wear when he was teaching. And the tiny socks and shoes.

When he got to the pants, he pulled out Fred's wallet and took out his ATM card.

He put the combination lock in his pocket and rushed out to the woman at the front counter. She handed him Fred's application form. They didn't say a word. Everything was all arranged ahead of time.

On his application form, Fred had written:

Bank ___KITTENS Bank_____

Your PIN at the ATM of your bank ___3141___

He drove down to KITTENS Bank and put Fred's card in the ATM and entered ③①④①. In 30 seconds, he had emptied out Fred's account.

Meanwhile, Fred, who was now penniless, had gone into the gym for his free class. *I must be early,* he thought. *There is no one else here.*

He sat on the floor and waited. In the dust on the floor he drew the numbers that add to 15:

$$
\begin{array}{cccc}
6 & 7 & 8 & 9 \\
+\ 9 & +\ 8 & +\ 7 & +\ 6 \\
\hline
15 & 15 & 15 & 15
\end{array}
$$

Dust? Fred thought. *A gym that was used wouldn't have a dusty floor with all the people running around on it.*

Fred walked out to the front counter. The woman was not there. He walked back into the locker room to talk to the attendant. He was gone.

Your Turn to Play

1. $6 + 9 = ?$
2. $7 + 8 = ?$
3. Guess what the rule is for this function:

    $4 \rightarrow 2$

    $8 \rightarrow 6$

    $9 \rightarrow 7$

    $20 \rightarrow 18$

    $85 \rightarrow 83$

4. Here is a harder one to guess:

· · · · · · · ANSWERS · · · · · · ·

1. 6 + 9 = 15

2. 7 + 8 = 15

3.   4 ➡ 2

       8 ➡ 6   The rule for this function is

       9 ➡ 7   subtract 2.

     20 ➡ 18   In algebra, we will write this

     85 ➡ 83   rule as $x ➡ x - 2$.

4.   This is called a **right angle** ☞

Squares have four right angles.

       So do rectangles.

This function counts the number of right angles.

 ➡ 1    ➡ 1

➡ 2   ➡ 2

➡ 0   ➡ 0

 ➡ 2

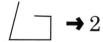 ➡ 6   ➡ 2

Chapter Ten
At the Bank

His clothes were scattered on the locker room floor. His locker door was open. The combination lock was gone.

Fred thought that a janitor had been cleaning each of the lockers and just hadn't had the opportunity to put his clothes back in his locker. He took off his over-sized gym clothes and hung them neatly in his locker and put on his regular clothes.

He noticed that his wallet had fallen out of his pants' pocket. He picked it up and put it back into his pocket. It felt a little bit lighter, but Fred figured that was because he had spent all of his dollar bills.[*]

He went into the bathroom to use the mirror to put on his bow tie. He was too short to use the dirty mirror that was over the sink.

Putting his bow tie in his pocket, he headed outside.

There was a big sign in front of the building.

---

[*] Fred got half of this right: *Be as cunning as serpents and yet as harmless as doves.*

I've got to get to the bank to get some more money Fred thought. Even though Fred had been employed for years as a teacher at KITTENS University, he didn't have any credit cards. The banks refused to issue credit cards to five-year-olds. He paid cash or wrote a check for everything he purchased. So Fred needed some cash.

There was a long line of students at the bank. Since the university president had canceled classes, they were there to get money so they could spend the day shopping.

Fred went around to the back of the building to use the ATM. He was glad that he didn't need to stand in line to wait for a teller. When he got to the ATM, he pulled out his wallet and discovered that his ATM card was missing. *It must have dropped out of my wallet when the janitor was cleaning the lockers* he thought.

Fred went around to the front of the building and waited in line with the students.

The line moved quickly since everyone was there for the same reason. The teller had a big sack of cash and was handing out the shopping money.*

When it got to be Fred's turn, he pushed a chair up to the teller and stood on it so that the teller could see him.

"Hi! Professor Gauss," she said. She was one of Fred's students. "What can I do for you?"

"I'd like $20 from my account, please," said Fred. (Fred always said "please" and "thank you.")

Fred knew that he had $560 in his account, and withdrawing $20 would leave $540.

$$
\begin{array}{r}
560 \\
-20 \\
\hline
540
\end{array}
$$

The teller checked the computer and said, "I'm afraid you don't have enough money in your account to withdraw $20. My computer says that about a half hour ago you went to the ATM and withdrew $560."

---

* At the end of the day, the merchants would come to the bank and deposit that money.

Fred quickly did the math:

$560   was in my account

− $560   withdrawn

$0   nothing in the account!

Fred couldn't imagine how that happened. A half hour ago he was sitting on the gym floor writing

6	7	8	9
+ 9	+ 8	+ 7	+ 6
15	15	15	15

in the dust on the floor. He couldn't have been at the ATM.

Fred thanked the teller and hopped off the chair. He pushed the chair back to where he had found it.

Fred left the bank and stood in the sunshine. He thought of heading back to his office and seeing Kingie. He would talk over his financial situation with his doll. It was early in February, and Fred's next paycheck would be at the beginning of March.

"Oh, no!" Fred exclaimed aloud. Several of the students who were still waiting in line outside the bank looked at Fred.

Fred realized that Kingie wasn't at his office. He had left his doll in the room behind the classroom where they had taken off their mouse ears.

Fred ran to the Archimedes building, down the hallway, and into his giant classroom. He headed into the room behind the classroom. There was Kingie patiently waiting for him.

Dolls are very good at waiting.

Your Turn to Play

Kingie had been creating functions for Fred to guess.

1. The first one that Kingie thought of was:

$3 \rightarrow 6$ $8 \rightarrow 16$

$5 \rightarrow 10$ $9 \rightarrow 18$

$2 \rightarrow 4$ $1{,}000 \rightarrow 2{,}000$

What is the rule for this function?

2. The second function that Kingie created was really easy. What is the rule?

Kansas $\rightarrow$ art

$4 \rightarrow$ art

the university president's left foot $\rightarrow$ art

$\sqrt{99} \rightarrow$ art

pizza $\rightarrow$ art

3. The last function that Kingie thought of was harder:

$4 \rightarrow 1$	$288 \rightarrow 3$	$7777 \rightarrow 4$	$6 \rightarrow 1$
$10 \rightarrow 2$	$289 \rightarrow 3$	$5554 \rightarrow 4$	$24 \rightarrow 2$
$1{,}000{,}000 \rightarrow 7$	$1 \rightarrow 1$		$4321 \rightarrow 4$

· · · · · · · **ANSWERS** · · · · · · ·

1. The rule for Kingie's first function was *Take the number and double it.*

In algebra, it is sometimes written as x ➜ 2x.

2. Kingie loves art. If you have ever seen some of his paintings, you can see that he has a real talent.

Kingie's Drawing

Fred's Drawing

The rule for Kingie's second function was *Art—no matter what is on the left side of the arrow.*

This is called a **constant function**.

3. The rule for Kingie's third function was *Count the number of digits in the number.*

Chapter Eleven
Fred's Budget

Fred gave Kingie a big hug. Kingie told him that he didn't mind waiting. The only thing that he didn't like is being in a room with a cat who might use him as a cat toy. Kingie didn't want to be torn to shreds.

Fred picked up Kingie, and together they headed back to Fred's office.

As they went, Fred said, "I'm afraid I've got some bad news to tell you."

Kingie was silent. He was listening hard. He was hoping that Fred wasn't going to announce that he was getting another cat.

Fred continued, "I think I am broke. I don't have any money in my wallet and the balance in my bank account is $0. I get paid on the first of each month, so we have about three weeks with no money."

Kingie giggled.

"Why are you giggling?" Fred asked. "I thought this would be really bad news."

Hee! Hee!

Kingie explained, "Three weeks without spending any money won't be that difficult. You don't pay any rent since we live in your university office. You never seem to eat, so we don't need grocery money. The only clothing you seem to buy are bow ties that you wear when you are teaching. You have a zillion of them, so you can go three weeks without buying another one."

Kingie was right about the costs of housing, food, and clothing. There were actually only two real items in Fred's budget.

Fred received his $500 teaching salary on the first work day of each month, so he put a check for $50 in the Sunday school offering on the first Sunday of each month. He was the only five-year-old in his class who contributed by check.

The only other item in his budget was buying books. His office walls were filled with

 books—most of which he had already read at least once. "What am I going to do about reading?" Fred asked. Little drops of sweat were forming on his forehead. The thought of not reading put Fred in a panic.

Fred imagined . . .

One day without reading :

Brain begins to feel dull.
Life seems a bit gray.
Start to feel dumb.

Two days without reading :

Difficulty forming new thoughts.
Becomes hard to read street signs.
Drooling begins.

Three days without reading :

This was too horrible to contemplate. Fred had once been at a lunch with a bunch of adults who were in the three-days-without-reading category. Their conversation was limited to:

(1) My trip to Arizona. A complete description of all the bad things that happened on that trip.

(2) The weather.

(3) What I saw on television.

(4) My kids.

(5) Sports.

(6) My health problems.

Fred did a <u>A Row of Practice</u> just to make sure his brain was still working. (You are encouraged to do this row also.)

$$
\begin{array}{cccccccc}
5 & 11 & 7 & 3 & 6 & 5 & 4 & 38 \\
+\ 6 & -\ 7 & +\ 8 & +\ 8 & +\ 9 & +\ 8 & +\ 7 & +\ 2 \\
\hline
11 & 4 & 15 & 11 & 15 & 13 & 11 & 40
\end{array}
$$

"You do have a library card," Kingie pointed out.

"Oh," said Fred. He had completely forgotten about that. When people are in a panic, they lose their ability to think as their IQ drops to that of a duck.

"Yes!" said Fred as he pulled his library card out of his wallet. "How obvious!"

The card was made out of stainless steel. Fred had used his regular library card so frequently that every month or so it would wear out. The library had finally issued him a metal library card so that they wouldn't have to keep replacing it. Very few readers earn a metal library card.

Fred danced around the room waving his card.

No longer in a panic, Fred could think straight. He gathered up the books that needed to go back to the library and headed out the door, past the nine vending machines in the hallway (5 on one side and 4 on the other), down two flights of stairs and out into the sunshine.

Your Turn to Play

1. If yesterday was Monday, what day will tomorrow be?

2. If last month was May, what will the month after this month be?

3. What is the natural number that comes right after 999? (The natural numbers are {1, 2, 3, 4, . . . }.)

4.   15

    $\underline{-\ 7}$

5. Find a number x such that x + x = 18.

6. 6 ducks + 5 ducks = ?

7. $6\pi + 5\pi$ = ? π is the Greek letter pi.

8. What is the cardinality of {9, π, 73}?

9. This is a function. What is the rule?

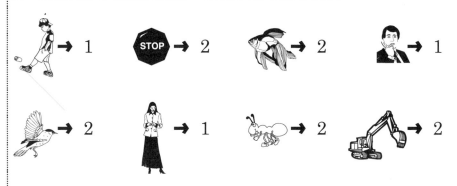

·······ANSWERS·······

1. If yesterday was Monday, what day will tomorrow be?

Sunday
Monday
Tuesday   If yesterday was Monday
Wednesday   then today will be Tuesday, and
Thursday   tomorrow will be Wednesday.
Friday
Saturday

2. January
February
March
April
May   If last month was May,
June   then this month will be June,
July   and next month will be July.

3. The natural number that comes right after 999 is 1,000. $999 + 1 = 1,000$

4. $$\begin{array}{r} 15 \\ -\ 7 \\ \hline 8 \end{array}$$

5. If x is 9, then $x + x = 18$.

6. 6 ducks + 5 ducks = 11 ducks

7. $6\pi + 5\pi = 11\pi$

8. The cardinality of $\{9, \pi, 73\}$ is 3. That is the number of elements in that set.

9. The rule for that function is: *If it is a human, then assign the number 1. Otherwise, assign the number 2.*

Chapter Twelve
To the Library

Returning a bunch of books that you have enjoyed reading to the library is a happy thing. Fred broke into song.

Borrowed Books

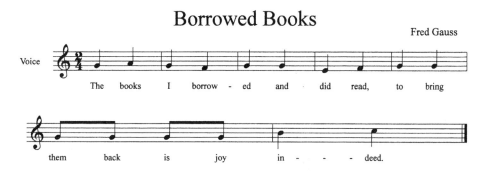

Fred Gauss

Voice

The books I borrow - ed and did read, to bring
them back is joy in - - - deed.

Fred's arms were too short to carry all the books he was returning to the library. He had discovered a different way to carry them. When the librarian first saw him do this, she said, "Fred, now you are using your head."

What was even more fun than bringing back books was the thought of discovering new books to read.

After he returned the books, he raced off to the library shelves to explore.

Sometimes, Fred would explore the chemistry books. Sometimes, the astronomy books. Sometimes, the great novels of Western literature.

A couple of years ago when Fred was three, he wanted to just pick a book at random. He shut his eyes and twirled around and walked.

With his unique nose, he learned that he shouldn't have done that. He got stuck in the wall, and the librarian had to come and pull him out.

But he was older now, and he didn't do that anymore. Five-year-olds are a lot more mature than three-year-olds.

After Fred dropped off the books that he was returning, he saw a sign.

Such beautiful handwriting, Fred thought. *I wish I could write that well.*

Then he thought about the fact that he could only check out 17 books. He knew that when the computers are down, the librarians have to write down everything on paper: the name of the person checking out the books and the titles of each of the books. That takes a lot longer than using the computer.

Fred knew that he had to choose his 17 books very carefully.

Seventeen. That's a very special number for students learning their addition tables. For many people it is their favorite number.

Why? Because there is only one addition fact to memorize: $8 + 9 = 17$. That's it.

When you learned the numbers that add to 11, you had to memorize:

$$\begin{array}{cccc} 2 & 3 & 4 & 5 \\ +\ 9 & +\ 8 & +\ 7 & +\ 6 \\ \hline 11 & 11 & 11 & 11 \end{array}$$ Four facts to learn.

(Nobody has to memorize $1 + 10 = 11$.)

When you learned the numbers that add to 13, you had to memorize:

$$\begin{array}{ccc} 4 & 5 & 6 \\ +\ 9 & +\ 8 & +\ 7 \\ \hline 13 & 13 & 13 \end{array}$$ Three facts to learn.

(Nobody has to memorize $2 + 11 = 13$ since if you know that $2 + 1 = 3$, then

$$\begin{array}{c} 2 \\ +\ 11 \\ \hline 13 \end{array}\quad \text{is obvious.})$$

When you learned the numbers that add to 15, you had to memorize:

$$9 \qquad 7$$
$$+\ 6 \qquad +\ 8$$
$$15 \qquad 15$$

Two facts to learn.

(Nobody has to memorize 3 + 12 = 15 since if you know that 3 + 2 = 5, then

$$3$$
$$+\ 12$$
$$15$$

is obvious.)

But with 17, there is only one fact to learn:

$$8$$
$$+\ 9$$
$$17$$

Only one fact to learn.

(Nobody has to memorize 6 + 11 = 17 since if you know that 6 + 1 = 7, then

$$6$$
$$+\ 11$$
$$17$$

is obvious.)

Fred wondered if that was the reason that the librarian with the pretty handwriting had chosen 17 as the checkout limit.

At the age of five, Fred did not know everything about everything. There was so much to learn. Because he could only take out 17 books today, Fred decided to limit himself to two different topics: 8 books on one topic and 9 books on the other.

He opened the dictionary at random to pick his first topic: macronutrient = *parts of food needed in large amounts, such as protein, carbohydrates, and fats.*

He had seen the words *protein, carbohydrate,* and *fat* on the labels of food packages, but Fred couldn't tell you what a protein was if it came up to him, and he put it on the barbecue.

Your Turn to Play

1. How many things wrong can you spot about this illustration?

2. What number doubled gives you 14? (Hint: When Fred taught this, he mentioned a fortnight.)

3. What number doubled gives you 16? (Hint: When Fred taught this, he and Kingie pretended they were cartoon characters with four fingers on each hand.)

4.   17
    − 8

5. Guess the rule for the function

January ➜ March	13 ➜ 15	Thursday ➜ Saturday
Washington ➜ Jefferson	Two o'clock ➜ Four o'clock	
B ➜ D Ford ➜ Reagan	A ➜ C	999 ➜ 1001
Mercury ➜ Earth	10 a.m. ➜ noon	Venus ➜ Mars

. . . . **ANSWERS** . . . .

1.

   i) Human hands and legs

   ii) Shoes

   iii) Eyebrows

   iv) Clothes

   v) It is not a barbecue but a pot

   vi) Using a spoon

   vii) Standing on two legs

2. A fortnight is 14 days, which is two 7-day weeks. Double 7 and you get 14.

3.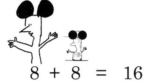

   $$8 + 8 = 16$$

4.
$$
\begin{array}{r}
17 \\
-\ 8 \\
\hline
9
\end{array}
\quad \text{since } 8 + 9 = 17
$$

5. The rule for this function is *advance two*. (There are many different ways you might have expressed this.)

Small astronomy lesson:

The list of planets around our sun: Mercury

Venus

Earth

Mars

Jupiter

Saturn

Uranus

Neptune

(Pluto used to be considered a planet. It no longer is.)

Chapter Thirteen
Picking a Topic to Read About

With a checkout limit of 17 books, Fred wanted to pick 8 books on one topic and 9 books on another topic. He had stuck his finger at random in the dictionary and decided that his first topic would be macronutrients. He went to the biology section of the library and chose:

Prof. Eldwood's *Guide to Protein*
Prof. Eldwood's *Guide to Carbohydrates*
Prof. Eldwood's *Guide to Fats*
Prof. Eldwood's *Guide to Protein and Carbohydrates*
Prof. Eldwood's *Guide to Protein and Fats*
Prof. Eldwood's *Guide to Carbohydrates and Fats*
Prof. Eldwood's *Guide to Protein, Carbohydrates, and Fats*
Prof. Eldwood's *Guide to Macronutrients*

With those eight books, Fred hoped to learn a lot about macronutrients.

The old finger-in-the-dictionary trick was one of many ways that Fred used to pick a topic.

✓ Sometimes he would hear about a topic that he knew very little about. Once Alexander mentioned to him the Hanging Gardens of Babylon—one of the Seven Wonders of the Ancient World. Fred got excited about this and read a lot about the Hanging Gardens, which were rooftop gardens irrigated by pumps from the Euphrates River. Later, he read about the other wonders of the ancient world.

✓ Sometimes Fred would find an author he liked, such as C. S. Lewis or M. Scott Peck, and then he would read everything that author had written.

✓ Sometimes he would read something in one book that would make him want to learn more about the topic. In Dr. Schmidt's *Life of Fred: Geometry* book, Fred came across this list: Affenpinscher, Afghan Hound, African Wild Dog, Ainu Dog, Airedale Terrier, Akbash Dog, Akita Inu, Alapaha Blue Blood Bulldog, Alaskan Husky, Alaskan Klee Kai, Alaskan Malamute, Alopekis, Alpine Dachsbracke, American Bandogge Mastiff, American Black and Tan Coonhound, American Blue Gascon Hound, American Bulldog, American Cocker Spaniel, American Crested Sand Terrier, American Eskimo Dog, American Foxhound, American Hairless Terrier, American Mastiff, American Pit Bull Terrier, American Staffordshire Terrier, American Staghound, American Toy Terrier, American Water Spaniel, American White Shepherd, Anatolian Shepherd Dog, Anglos-Françaises, Anglos-Françai Grand, Anglos-Français de Moyenne Venerie, Anglos-Françaises de Petite Venerie, Appenzell Mountain Dog, Ariegeois, Armant, Aryan Molossus, Argentine Dogo, Arubian Cunucu Dog, Australian Bandog, Australian Bulldog, Australian Cattle Dog, Australian Kelpie, Australian Shepherd, Australian Stumpy Tail Cattle Dog, Australian Terrier, Austrian Brandlbracke, Austrian Shorthaired Pinscher, Azawakh, Banjara Greyhound, Barbet, Basenji, Basset Artesien Normand, Basset Hound, Bavarian Mountain Hound, Beagle, Beagle Harrier, Bearded Collie, Beauceron, Bedlington Terrier, Bedouin Shepherd Dog, Belgian Griffons, Belgian Mastiff, Belgian Shepherd Groenendael, Belgian Shepherd Laekenois, Belgian Shepherd Malinois, Belgian Shorthaired Pointer, Belgrade Terrier, Bergamasco, Berger des Picard, Berger des Pyrénées, Berger Du Languedoc, Bernese Mountain Dog, Bichon Frise, Bichon Havanais, Bichon/Yorkie, Billy, Black and Tan Coonhound, Black Forest Hound, Black Mouth Cur, Black Russian Terrier, Bleus De Gascogne, Bloodhound, Blue Heeler, Blue Lacy, Bluetick Coonhound, Boerboel, Bohemian Terrier, Bolognese, Border Collie, Border Terrier, Borzoi, Boston Terrier, Bouvier des Flanders, Bouvier de Ardennes, Boxer, Boykin Spaniel, Bracco Italiano, Braque D' Ariege, Braque D' Auvergne, Braque Du Bourbonnais, Braque Dupuy, Braque Saint-Germain, Braques Françaises, Brazilian Terrier, Briard, Brittany Spaniel, Briquet, Broholmer, Brussels Griffon, Bull Boxer, Bull Terrier, Bulldog, Bullmastiff, Cairn Terrier, Cajun Squirrel Dog, Canary Dog, Canaan Dog, Cane Corso Italiano, Canis Panther, Canoe Dog, Cão da Serra da Estrela, Carlin Pinscher, Caravan Hound, Carolina Dog, Carpathian Sheepdog, Catahoula Bulldog, Catahoula Leopard Dog, Catalan Sheepdog, Caucasian Ovtcharka, Cardigan Welsh Corgi, Cavalier King Charles Spaniel, Central Asian Ovtcharka, Cesky Fousek, Cesky Terrier, Chart Polski, Chesapeake Bay Retriever, Chien D' Artois, Chien De L' Atlas, Chiens Francaises, Chihuahua, Chin, Chinese Chongqing Dog, Chinese Crested, Chinese Foo Dog, Chinese Shar-Pei, Chinook, Chippiparai, Chortaj, Chow Chow, Cirneco Dell 'Etna, Clumber Spaniel, Cockapoo, Cocker Spaniel, Collie, Combai, Continental Toy Spaniel, Corgi, Coton De Tulear, Cretan Hound, Croatian Sheepdog, Curly-Coated Retriever, Cypro Kukur, Czechoslovakian Wolfdog, Czesky Terrier, Dachshund, Dalmatian, Dandie Dinmont Terrier, Danish Broholmer, Danish/Swedish Farm Dog, Danish Chicken Dog, Deutsche Bracke, Deutscher Wachtelhund, Dingo, Doberman Pinscher, Dogo Argentino, Dogue Brasileiro, Dogue de Bordeaux, Dorset Olde Tyme Bulldogge, Drentse Patrijshond, Drever, Dunker, Dutch Shepherd Dog, Dutch Smoushond, East-European Shepherd, East Russian Coursing Hounds, East Siberian Laika, Elkhound, English Bulldog, English Cocker Spaniel, English Coonhound, English Foxhound, English Pointer, English Setter, English Shepherd, English Springer Spaniel, English Toy Spaniel, Entelbucher Sennenhund, Epagneul Francais, Epagneul Pont-Audemer, Epagneuls Picardies, Eskimo Dog, Estonian Hound, Estrela Mountain Dog, Eurasier, Farm Collie, Fauves De Bretagne, Feist, Field Spaniel, Fila Brasileiro, Finnish Hound, Finnish Lapphund, Finnish Spitz, Flat-Coated Retriever, Foxhound, Fox Terrier, French Brittany Spaniel, French Bulldog, French Mastiff, Galgo Espanol, Gascons-Saintongeois, German Hunt Terrier, German Longhaired Pointer, German Pinscher, German Sheeppoodle, German Shepherd Dog, German Shorthaired Pointer, German Spitz, German Wirehaired Pointer, German Wolfspitz, Giant Schnauzer, Glen of Imaal Terrier, Golden Retriever, Goldendoodle, Gordon Setter, Gran Mastin de Borinquen, Grand Anglo-Français, Great Dane, Great Pyrenees, Greater Swiss Mountain Dog, Greek Hound, Greek Sheepdog, Greenland Dog, Greyhound, Griffon Nivernais, Griffons Vendéens, Groenendael, Grosser Müünsterlääander Vorstehhund, Guatemalan Bull Terrier, Hairless Khala, Halden Hound, Hamiltonstovare, Hanoverian Hound, Harlequin Pinscher, Harrier, Havanese, Hawaiian Poi Dog, Hellenikos Ichnilatis, Hellenikos Poimenikos, Hertha Pointer, Himalayan Sheepdog, Hokkaido Dog, Hovawart, Hygenhund, Hungarian Greyhound, Hungarian Kuvasz, Hungarian Puli, Husky, Ibizan Hound, Icelandic Sheepdog, Inca Hairless Dog, Irish Glen Imaal Terrier, Irish Red and White Setter, Irish Setter, Irish Staffordshire Bull Terrier, Irish Terrier, Irish Water Spaniel, Irish Wolfhound, Italian Greyhound, Italian Spinoni, Jack Russell Terrier, Japanese Spaniel, Japanese Spitz, Japanese Terrier, Jindo, Kai Dog, Kangal Dog, Kangaroo Dog, Kanni, Karabash, Karakachan, Karelian Bear Dog, Karelian Bear Laika, Karelo-Finnish Laika, Keeshond, Kelb Tal-Fenek, Kemmer Feist, Kerry Beagle, Kerry Blue Terrier, King Charles Spaniel, King Shepherd, Komondor, Kooikerhondje, Koolie, Krasky Ovcar, Kromfohrlläänder, Kugsha Dog, Kunming Dog, Kuvasz, Labradoodle, Labrador Husky, Labrador Retriever, Lagotto Romagnolo, Lakeland Terrier, Lancashire Heeler, Landseer, Lapinporokoira, Lapphunds, Larson Lakeview Bulldogge, Latvian Hound, Leonberger, Leopard Cur, Levesque, Lhasa Apso, Lithuanian Hound, Llewellin Setter, Louisiana Catahoula Leopard Dog, Lowchen, Lucas Terrier, Lundehund, Lurcher, Magyar Agar, Mahratta Greyhound, Majestic Tree Hound, Maltese, Malti-Poo, Manchester Terrier, Maremma Sheepdog, Markiesje, Mastiff, McNab, Mexican Hairless, Mi-Ki, Middle Asian Ovtcharka, Miniature Australian Shepherd, Miniature Bull Terrier, Miniature American Eskimo, Miniature Pinscher, Miniature Poodle, Miniature Schnauzer, Mioritic Sheepdog, Moscow Toy Terrier, Moscow Vodolaz, Moscow Watchdog, Mountain Cur, Mountain View Cur, Mucuchies, Mudhol Hound, Mudi, Neapolitan Mastiff, Nebolish Mastiff, Mutt, Nenets Herding Laika, New Guinea Singing Dog, New Zealand Huntaway, Newfoundland, Norbottenspets, Norfolk Terrier, North American Miniature Australian Shepherd, Northeasterly Hauling Laika, Northern Inuit Dog, Norwegian Elkhound, Norwegian Buhund, Norwich Terrier, Nova Scotia Duck-Tolling Retriever, Olde Boston Bulldogge, Old Danish Bird Dog, Old English Mastiff, Old English Sheepdog, Old-Time Farm Shepherd, Olde English Bulldogge, Original English Bulldogge, Otterhound, Owczarek Podhalanski, Papillon, Pashmi Hound, Patterdale Terrier, Pekepoo, Pekingese, Pembroke Welsh Corgi, Perdiguero Portugueso, Perdiguero de Burgos, Perdiguero Navarro, Perro Cimarron, Perro de Pastor Mallorquin, Perro de Presa Canario, Perro de Presa Mallorquin, Perro Ratonero Andaluz, Peruvian Inca Orchid, Petit Basset Griffon Vendéen, Petit Brabancon, Pharaoh Hound, Pit Bull Terrier, Plott Hound, Podengo Portuguesos Grande, Podengo Portuguesos Méédio, Podengo Portuguesos Pequeno, Podenco

Ibicenco, Pointer, Poitevin, Polish Hound, Polski Owczarek Nizinny, Polski Owczarek Podhalanski, Pomeranian, Poodle, Poos, Porcelaine, Portuguese Podengo Pequeno, Portuguese Water Dog, Portuguese Rabbit Dog, Potsdam Greyhound, Prazsky Krysavik, Presa Canarios, Pudelpointer, Pug, Puli, Pumi, Pyrenean Mastiff, Pyrenean Mountain Dog, Queensland Heeler, Rafeiro do Alentejo, Rajapalyam, Rampur Greyhound, Rastreador Brasileiro, Rat Terrier, Redbone Coonhound, Rhodesian Ridgeback, Rottweiler, Rough Collie, Rumanian Sheepdog, Russian Bear Schnauzer, Russian Harlequin Hound, Russian Hound, Russian Spaniel, Russian Tsvetnaya Bolonka, Russian Wolfhound, Russo-European Laika, Saarlooswolfhond, Sabuesos Espanoles, Sage Ashayeri, Sage Koochee, Sage Mazandarani, Saint Bernard, Saluki, Samoyed, Sanshu Dog, Sarplaninac, Schapendoes, Schillerstovare, Schipperke, Schnauzers, Schnoodle, Scotch Collie, Scottish Deerhound, Scottish Terrier (Scottie), Sealydale Terrier, Sealyham Terrier, Segugios Italianos, Shar-Pei, Shetland Sheepdog (Sheltie), Shiba Inu, Shichon, Shih-Tzu, Shika Inus, Shikoku, Shiloh Shepherd, Siberian Husky, Siberian Laikas, Silken Windhound, Silky Terrier, Simaku, Skye Terrier, Sloughi, Slovensky Cuvac, Smalandsstovare, Small Greek Domestic Dog, Smooth Collie, Smooth Fox Terrier, Soft Coated Wheaten Terrier, South Russian Ovtcharka, Spanish Mastiff, Spanish Water Dog, Spinone Italiano, Springer Spaniel, Stabyhoun, Staffordshire Bull Terrier, Staghound, Standard American Eskimo, Standard Poodle, Standard Schnauzer, Stephens Stock, Stichelhaar, Strellufstover, Styrian Roughhaired Mountain Hound, Sussex Spaniel, Swedish Lapphund, Swedish Vallhund, Swiss Shorthaired Pinscher, Swiss Laufhunds, Tahltan Bear Dog, Taigan, Tasy, Teddy Roosevelt Terrier, Telomian, Tenterfield Terrier, Tepeizeuintli, Thai Ridgeback, The Carolina Dog, Tibetan Mastiff, Tibetan Spaniel, Tibetan Terrier, Titan Terrier, Tosa Inu, Toy American Eskimo, Toy Fox Terrier, Toy German Spitz, Toy Manchester Terrier, Toy Poodle, Transylvanian Hounds, Treeing Tennessee Brindle, Treeing Walker Coonhound, Tuareg Sloughi, Tyroler Bracke, Valley Bulldog, Vasgotaspets, Victorian Bulldog, Villano de Las Encartaciones, Vizsla, Volpino Italiano, Vucciriscu, Weimaraner, Welsh Corgi, Welsh Sheepdog, Welsh Springer Spaniel, Welsh Terrier, West Highland White Terrier, West Russian Coursing Hound, West Siberian Laika, Westphalian Dachsbracke, Wetterhoun, Wheaten Terrier, Whippet, White German Shepherd, Wirehaired Fox Terrier, Wirehaired Pointing Griffon, Wirehaired Vizsla, Wolf Hybred, Xoloitzcuintle, Yorkshire Terrier, and Yugoslavian Hounds.

Fred realized that he couldn't tell an Anatolian Shepherd Dog from a hot dog.

Fred went to the dog section of the library and took out nine dog books:

Prof. Eldwood's *History of Dogs*
Prof. Eldwood's *Dogs in Art*
Prof. Eldwood's *Why Dogs Have Hair*
Prof. Eldwood's *Dogs Who Look Like People*
Prof. Eldwood's *Dogs That Don't Shed*
Prof. Eldwood's *Dogs That Do Shed*
Prof. Eldwood's *Relations Between Dogs and Cats*
Prof. Eldwood's *Why Dogs Don't Marry*
Prof. Eldwood's *Geometry Books that Mention Dogs*

Fred checked his 17 books out of the library and deposited them in the KITTENS campus mail. They would be delivered to his office before he could get there. Besides, 17 books were too heavy to carry on the top of his head.

Fred stepped out into the cool Kansas air. It was ten minutes after twelve.

12:10 p.m.

Fred wasn't hungry yet. He wondered how he might spend the afternoon.

It had been two hours since he had read the newspaper. He picked up the noon edition.

THE KITTEN Caboodle

The Official Campus Newspaper of KITTENS University   Tuesday noon   10¢

exclusive

Dogs Need New Homes

KANSAS: The KITTENS Animal Shelter announced an hour ago that they had too many dogs.

Needs adoption

"We just don't have enough cages to keep them all," said Mrs. Hund, head of the Animal Shelter. "We receive all the dogs that people turn in to us and try to give them a nice place to stay. We hope that people who want a dog will come and adopt one."

Mrs. Hund pointed to a chart on the wall. In November the shelter received 60 dogs and only 30 dogs were adopted by the public.

In December the shelter received 50 dogs and the public only adopted 20.

In January many people had spent so much money on Christmas presents that they could not afford to keep their dogs.

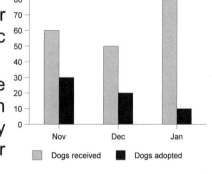

"It's cruel," said Mrs. Hund, "to keep so many dogs in so few cages. Because we love them so much, we can't let them suffer. Today at 1 p.m. we will have to put 30 of them to sleep."

Fred was in a panic. He was only five years old, and he didn't realize that animal shelters often have to euthanize* dogs and cats when not enough people come to adopt them.

The KITTEN Caboodle was describing a real need. Some other newspapers just try to sell papers by making everyday things into emotional headlines:

Politician Lies to Public!

Woman Burns Her Finger in Kitchen!

Dog Barks in Philadelphia!

Your Turn to Play

1. (This question is especially good for anyone who may want to be an art major in college.)

Make a chart like the one in the article on the previous page. Make it for the months of October, November, and December. For October, the data are 50 pies eaten, 10 pounds gained. For November, 20 pies eaten, 5 pounds gained. For December, 80 pies eaten, 30 pounds gained.

2. How many digits does the number 62,000 have?

3. $6x + 9x = ?$

4. 8 pianos + 9 pianos $= ?$

---

* YOU-than-ize   Euthanize = mercy killing. To put to death painlessly. If you become a veterinarian, part of your job may be to euthanize dogs and cats that are in pain and are so sick that they will never get well.

. . . . ANSWERS . . . .

1.

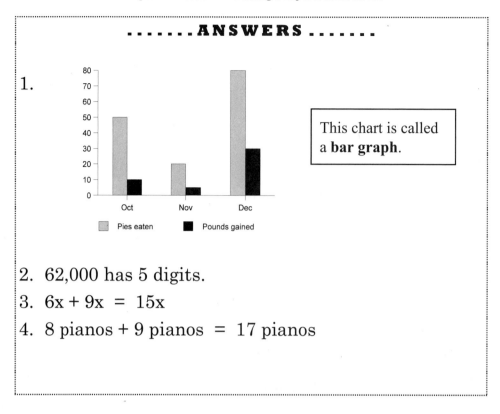

This chart is called
a **bar graph**.

2. 62,000 has 5 digits.

3. 6x + 9x = 15x

4. 8 pianos + 9 pianos = 17 pianos

small essay

Every Job

Every occupation has its good parts and its bad parts. But what is fun for one person may be a real pain for another.

One person may enjoy working in a hospital helping people heal. Another person might not like dealing with sick people.

One person might enjoy sitting in a small room in front of a computer writing about Fred (I do!) and others might like bullfighting.

One purpose of childhood is to start to figure out what things you, yourself, like to do.

end of small essay

Chapter Fourteen
To the Animal Shelter

It took Fred 15 minutes from the time he read the article to:

    1. Find the address of the animal shelter in the phonebook. (123 Katze Street)

    2. Look on a map to determine where 123 Katze Street is.

    3. Run a mile from the library to 123 Katze Street.

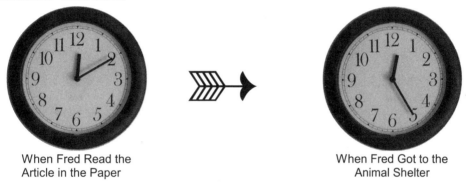

When Fred Read the
Article in the Paper

When Fred Got to the
Animal Shelter

The paper said that at 1 p.m. they would be euthanizing 30 dogs, and Fred did not want to be late.

Fred ran inside. It was now 12:25. He had 35 minutes until one o'clock.

"Hello, little boy," said Mrs. Hund.

"I'd like to speak with Mrs. Hund, please," said Fred.

She pointed to her name tag.

> Mrs. Hund, Director
> KITTENS Animal Shelter

Fred was in such a panic, he had almost forgotten how to read.

"Dogs . . ." was all that Fred could blurt out.

"Where are your parents?" she asked. She was used to seeing parents come in with their little boys. She thought his parents were outside. It was a policy of the animal shelter not to have little kids wander around the shelter unsupervised.

Fred had been asked this question many times over the last five years. Rather than explaining that his mother is in Heaven, and that he hadn't seen his father in over four and a half years, Fred said, "I'm at the University."

Mrs. Hund laughed. "Four-year-olds are not students at the University."

"I'm not four. Many people think that because I am short. I'm really five years old. And I am not a student at KITTENS."

Fred showed Mrs. Hund his faculty card.

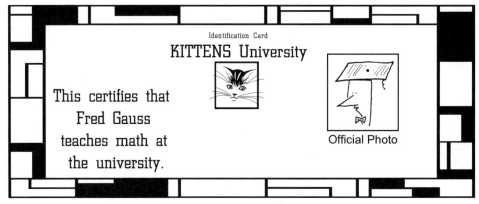

Identification Card
KITTENS University

This certifies that
Fred Gauss
teaches math at
the university.

Official Photo

Mrs. Hund didn't know what to say. She had heard that there was a five-year-old who was teaching mathematics at KITTENS, but she had thought that was just a joke.

"I'm here to adopt," Fred began.

"We're pretty busy right now," Mrs. Hund explained. "In about a half hour, we have 30 dogs that we need to put to sleep." She didn't use the word *euthanize* when talking to people who are three feet tall.

She handed him an application form to fill out and then headed into another room. Fred filled it out.

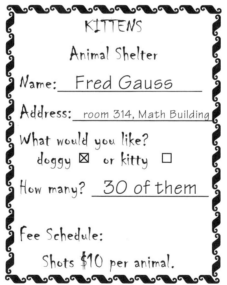

When Fred saw the Fee Schedule, he realized that it costs money to adopt a pet.

He added up 10 + 10 + 10 + 10 + 10 + 10 + 10 + 10 + 10 + 10 + 10 + 10 + 10 + 10 + 10 + 10 + 10 + 10 + 10 + 10 + 10 + 10 + 10 + 10 +

10 + 10 + 10 + 10, which is thirty 10s. (In later math, we will say that is, "30 times 10.")

The shots for 30 dogs will cost $300. He didn't have $300. In fact, Fred was penniless. He had spent all the money in his wallet at the gym, and his bank account had no money in it.

What am I going to do? Fred thought. *At one o'clock those dogs are toast.**

He thought of going to the bank to get a loan of $300 but remembered how long the line was. He had 35 minutes and didn't want to be standing in a bank line at one o'clock.

He ran back to his office.

From the animal shelter . . .

across campus . . .

to the math building . . .

up two flights of stairs . . .

down the hallway

passing 9 vending machines . . .

4 on the left and 5 on the right . . .

and opened his office door.

---

* *To be toast* means to be in real trouble. It has nothing to do with bread or with cooking. *To be toast* is an **idiom**. (ID-ee-um)

An idiom is an expression that means something other than what it says.
Make a bed doesn't mean to get out a hammer and nails and build a bed.
Catch fire doesn't mean to reach out and grab it.
To kick the bucket has nothing to do with feet or buckets.

Kingie was busy painting. He often did that when Fred was away at class.

Fred said, "I've got to borrow $300 in order to save the 30 dogs."

He headed to the phone on his desk to call Alexander.

He dialed. It rang. No answer.

He phoned Betty. It rang. No answer.

Your Turn to Play

1. Thirty 10s is the same as ten 30s.

Thirty rows of 10 chairs will seat the same number of people as ten rows of 30 chairs.

Here is the picture:

Later, when you learn about multiplication, we will write thirty 10s as 30×10.

30×10 gives the same answer as 10×30.

$30 \times 10 = 10 \times 30$.

This is an example of the commutative law of multiplication.

Your question: Fill in the blank: $5 + 7 = 7 + 5$ is an example of the _____ law of addition.

2. Is subtraction commutative?

3. Is putting on your shoes and socks commutative?

. . . . **ANSWERS** . . . .

1. $5 + 7 = 7 + 5$ is an example of the <u>commutative</u> law of addition.

So are . . . $3 + 9 = 9 + 3$

$2 + 4 = 4 + 2$

$7 + 1 = 1 + 7$

$389 + 16 = 16 + 389$

2. Does $8 - 3$ give the same answer as $3 - 8$? No.

If I have 8 jelly beans and eat 3 of them, I have 5 jelly beans left. $8 - 3 = 5$

If I have 3 jelly beans and eat 8 of them—that's crazy!

Subtraction is not commutative.

3. If you put on your socks and then put on your shoes, everything is fine.

If you first put on your shoes and then try to put on your socks, you are in **DEEP TROUBLE**.

These two things are not commutative.

Chapter Fifteen
Saving the Dogs

Fred didn't know who else to call. Darlene and Joe spent every dime they had the minute they got it.* They didn't know how to save.

Fred sat at his desk with his head in his hands.

Kingie heard a knock on the door. He put down his paintbrush, went to the door, and opened it.

"Here you are, Mr. Kingie," the delivery man said. He handed a wad of hundred dollar bills to Kingie.

Kingie tossed the money into his briefcase and went back to painting.

Fred looked in amazement. He couldn't believe what he was seeing.

"Where? What? How?" Fred sputtered.

---

* People who spend all their money the minute they get it are called spendthrifts. The other word for spendthrift is prodigal.

    In legal documents, you sometimes find spendthrift clauses.

    In one famous story, there was a prodigal son.

    In Life of Fred, there are Darlene and Joe.

Kingie set down his brush again and went over to Fred. Fred picked him up and put him on his desk so they could talk eye-to-eye.

Kingie began, "You go off to class each day to teach. The university pays you $500 a month. While you are teaching, I'm here at home painting."

"Yes," said Fred. "I think that is a very nice hobby."

Kingie ignored the interruption and continued, "Did you ever notice that even though I have been painting for years. . . ."

Fred interrupted again, "Yes, and getting better and better with all that practice."

Kingie repeated himself, "And did you ever notice that after all those years I don't have a pile of paintings here in the office?"

Fred shook his head. "Don't you just throw them away after you've finished them? That's what happens to most art that children do."

Kingie pointed to the painting he had been working on. "This isn't kid art. This is doll art. People love my work. I sell my paintings." He pointed to the briefcase full of money and asked, "How much would you like to borrow?"

Fred held up three fingers.

"Winter Scene"
by Kingie

Kingie hopped off the desk and went and pulled out three one hundred dollar bills.

It was 15 minutes to one. Fred had to hurry.

He headed out the door . . .
down the hallway . . .
past the 9 vending machines . . .
(4 on one side and 5 on the other)
down two flights of stairs . . .
across the campus . . .
to 123 Katze Street to the animal shelter.

12:45

He tried to hand Mrs. Hund the $300 and the application form. Out of breath, he said, "I'd like the 30 that were going to be euthanized."

"You are too late," Mrs. Hund said.

A thousand thoughts went through Fred's mind:

1. How could I be too late? It is five minutes to one.

2. Why didn't she wait till one?

3. The line from some famous poem: "Abandon hope, all you who enter here."

12:55

4. If only I had the $300 with me when I first came to this animal shelter, I could have saved them.

5. I don't normally carry $300 with me.

6. Were all the doggies as cute as the one they showed in the newspaper?

7. What do they do with the bodies of all those dead dogs?

8. 30 of them.

9. I'm glad I don't work in an animal shelter.

10. I know it is not cruel. There were too many dogs and not enough cages. They were unhappy, but they are not unhappy now.

11. I am unhappy.

Fred cried.

Mrs. Hund leaned over and put her hand on his shoulder. "It's okay. I'm sorry you were too late. Just five minutes ago. . . ."

Fred sobbed.

"Just five minutes ago, a tall fellow and his girlfriend, came in. They each adopted 15 of the dogs."

Mrs. Hund continued, "They went around to the back of the building to pick up their dogs. They said they were students at the university. Do you know them? Their names were Alexander and Betty."

Your Turn to Play

1. It's time to learn how to add two-digit numbers together.

    If you add 13 and 13, it looks like this:

$$\begin{array}{r} 13 \\ +\ 13 \\ \hline 26 \end{array}$$

You add the 3 + 3 and get 6.
You add the 1 + 1 and get 2.

If you add 12 and 37, it looks like this:

$$\begin{array}{r} 12 \\ +\ 37 \\ \hline 49 \end{array}$$

You add the 2 + 7 and get 9.
You add the 1 + 3 and get 4.

Your turn:

$$\begin{array}{r} 24 \\ +\ 23 \\ \hline \end{array}$$

2. You can also add three-digit numbers:

$$\begin{array}{r} 316 \\ +\ 482 \\ \hline \end{array}$$

.... ANSWERS ....

1.   24
     + 23
       47

You add the 4 + 3 and get 7.

You add the 2 + 2 and get 4.

(You first do the ones and then you do the tens. You work from right to left.)

2. You can add three-digit numbers also: 316
                                            + 482
                                              798

You add the 6 + 2 and get 8.

You add the 1 + 8 and get 9.

You add the 3 + 4 and get 7.

(You first do the ones, then the tens, then the hundreds. You work from right to left.)

I'm going to do a super big one just for fun:

873293045002
+ 124502721345   You start with the 2 + 5.
997795766347

Chapter Sixteen
Waiting for Dogs

Fred headed out the front door and around to the back of the animal shelter building. Betty and Alexander were standing there, but there were no dogs with them.

Fred ran up to them. His face was red from crying, and he had $300 in his hand.

Time Out!
Art in advertising

This is for art majors who will work in advertising.

If you want something to look big, you put it next to small things—like Fred's hand.
When Fred holds hundred dollar bills, they look huge.

When Alexander holds hundred dollar bills, you can hardly see them.

"Where are the dogs?" Fred asked.

Betty told him that the dogs were getting their shots. After that, they would get their dogs.

Fred put his money in his pocket.

Fred was curious and asked, "How are you going to carry that many dogs?"

He had done the math: If there are 30 dogs and each one weighs 20 pounds, then all 30 dogs would weigh 20 + 20 + 20 + 20 + 20 + 20 + 20 + 20 + 20 + 20 + 20 + 20 + 20 + 20 + 20 + 20 + 20 + 20 + 20 + 20 + 20 + 20 + 20 + 20 + 20 + 20 + 20 + 20 + 20 + 20 which is 600 pounds.*

Fred could do math, but he didn't know much about dogs.

Betty explained to him, "You don't have to carry dogs. They can walk."

Fred asked, "But if you let them walk, won't they run away?"

Betty held up 15 leashes that she had brought with her. Alexander held up another 15 leashes.

❀   ❀   ❀

Adding 14 + 14 is duck soup.**

$$\begin{array}{r} 14 \\ +\ 14 \\ \hline 28 \end{array}$$

But adding 15 leashes and 15 leashes isn't the same as adding 14 + 14.

---

* Later, when we do multiplication, we will write 30 twenties as 30 × 20.

** Duck soup = really easy to do. It is an idiom. *Duck soup* came into the English language around 1910.

WRONG
$$\begin{array}{r} 15 \\ + 15 \\ \hline 2_{10} \end{array}$$

Instead, you write the 0 and "carry the one." It looks like this:

right
$$\begin{array}{r} \overset{1}{}15 \\ + 15 \\ \hline 30 \end{array}$$

Here's another example:

right
$$\begin{array}{r} \overset{1}{}36 \\ + 27 \\ \hline 63 \end{array}$$

❁   ❁   ❁

Betty explained to Fred, "I know this seems silly—our getting thirty dogs from the animal shelter. We read in the KITTEN Caboodle newspaper about their putting these dogs to sleep and decided to help."

She told Fred how they got their checkbooks and headed to the animal shelter.

Fred figured out when everything happened.

noon
KITTEN Caboodle
published

12:10
Fred, Alexander, and
Betty read the paper

12:25
Fred got to the Animal
Shelter

12:30
Half past twelve
Fred headed back
to his office

12:35
Alexander and Betty
arrived at the shelter

12:45
A quarter to one
Alexander and Betty
filled out application
forms and paid for the
shots

12:55
Fred arrived back at the
shelter and was told,
"You are too late"

1:00
Fred, Alexander, and
Betty are in back of the
building waiting for the
dogs

The back door of the shelter opened. Mrs. Hund apologized to Betty and Alexander, "I'm sorry it took so long. Usually people adopt one dog at a time. Giving shots to 30 dogs has taken a little longer."

Your Turn to Play

Copy these on a piece of paper and answer them:

1. Easy addition

$$
\begin{array}{r} 15 \\ +\,82 \\ \hline \end{array}
\qquad
\begin{array}{r} 62 \\ +\,24 \\ \hline \end{array}
\qquad
\begin{array}{r} 80 \\ +\,17 \\ \hline \end{array}
$$

2. Medium difficulty

$$
\begin{array}{r} 16 \\ +\,45 \\ \hline \end{array}
\qquad
\begin{array}{r} 35 \\ +\,46 \\ \hline \end{array}
\qquad
\begin{array}{r} 87 \\ +\,8 \\ \hline \end{array}
$$

3. If you can get even one of these right, you are doing great.

$$
\begin{array}{r} 2348 \\ +\;\;463 \\ \hline \end{array}
\qquad
\begin{array}{r} 3 \\ 23 \\ +\,37 \\ \hline \end{array}
\qquad
\begin{array}{r} 3008 \\ +\quad 3 \\ \hline \end{array}
$$

......ANSWERS.......

1.

$$
\begin{array}{ccc}
15 & 62 & 80 \\
+\,82 & +\,24 & +\,17 \\
\hline
97 & 86 & 97
\end{array}
$$

2. In these problems, you need to "carry the one."

$$
\begin{array}{ccc}
\overset{1}{1}6 & \overset{1}{3}5 & \overset{1}{8}7 \\
+\,45 & +\,46 & +\,\ 8 \\
\hline
61 & 81 & 95
\end{array}
$$

3. The super-hard ones. Most people don't get many of these correct on their first try.

$$
\begin{array}{ccc}
2\overset{1\,1}{3}48 & 3 & 3\overset{1}{0}08 \\
+\ \ \ 463 & \overset{1}{2}3 & +\ \ \ \ 3 \\
\hline
2811 & +\,37 & 3011 \\
& \hline & \\
& 63 &
\end{array}
$$

Chapter Seventeen
On a Leash

Mrs. Hund led the first dog out, and Alexander put it on a leash. She led the second dog out, and Betty put it on a leash. Alexander put the third dog on a leash. Betty put the fourth dog on a leash.

First, second, third, fourth, . . . are ordinal numbers. They talk about the order in which things happen.

One, two, three, four, . . . are cardinal numbers. They are used for counting.

When the thirtieth (30th) dog was put on a leash, they had 30 dogs.

ordinal

cardinal

They headed down the street together.

$$
\begin{array}{r}
\overset{1}{15} \quad \leftarrow \text{Alexander's dogs} \\
15 \quad \leftarrow \text{Betty's dogs} \\
2 \quad \leftarrow \text{Alexander and Betty} \\
+\ \ 1 \quad \leftarrow \text{Fred} \\
\hline
33 \quad \quad \quad \quad \quad \quad \quad \quad
\end{array}
$$

Fred asked Betty if he could hold the leash of one of her dogs. Betty picked out the oldest, most gentle dog for Fred.

She didn't want to give him one of the bigger, more active dogs.

Fred had never had a dog on a leash before. He wondered if you had to steer it like a car. When the dog headed off to the right, Fred just followed it. It was almost as if Fred were on the leash and not the dog.

He thought of getting a saddle for the dog. Then he could ride it like a horse. But that wouldn't work because he didn't know how to ride a horse.

When the dog saw the other 29 dogs going down the street with Betty and Alexander, he ran to catch up with them. He pulled Fred along with him.

Dogs like to run in packs. They are much more sociable than cats.

Fred was starting to really like "his" dog. It really wasn't his dog. He was just pretending.

When he saw Alexander pet one of his dogs, Fred tried to pet the dog that Betty had lent him. He gave the dog one pat. Fred thought, *Do I have to wash my hands after touching a dog?*

Betty could see that Fred was trying really hard to work with the dog she had lent him. She asked, "Fred, would you like to name the dog?"

He was overjoyed. He dreamed of going to see Betty and her 15 dogs in her apartment, and one of those dogs would be special. It would be a dog he had named.

He asked the dog for a name. The dog said, "Ruff!"

Fred announced, "I think we should call this dog Ralph. He would like that."

Betty and Alexander giggled. They could see that Ralph was female.*

Fred gave Ralph another pat on the head.

They walked across the KITTENS campus, all 33 of them (30 dogs and 3 people).

When they got to the math building where Fred's office was, Fred looked up at Betty. She knew what Fred was thinking. She nodded and smiled.

Fred now owned a dog.

---

* Female = ♀ = girl/woman.
    Male = ♂ = boy/man.

"Come on Ralph," Fred said, and the pair of them headed up two flights of stairs, down the hallway, past the nine vending machines (four on one side and five on the other), and into his office.

Kingie was in the office doing his usual thing. Fred said, "Shut your eyes. I have a surprise for you."

Kingie shut his eyes, hoping that it wasn't another cat.

Ralph came up to Kingie and gave him a lick. Kingie tasted a little like butter.*

Kingie opened his eyes. A thousand thoughts went through Kingie's mind:

1. *It's not a cat. Thank Goodness.* ← That's a prayer.

2. *It's a dog! what am I in for?*

3. *It looks like a tame, nice, gentle dog.*

4. *This* *is better than this* .

5. *I wonder what Fred is going to do with a dog. He teaches all day long. Will I have to take care of it?*

---

* When Fred was four days old, he and his parents went to King of French Fries. The man who worked there gave Fred a free toy. It was Kingie. Kingie had some butter on him from the french fries. (The whole story is told in Chapters 5 and 6 of *Life of Fred: Calculus*.)

6. *Does Fred know how to take care of a dog? The nine books that he got out of the library won't help him at all.*

Prof. Eldwood's *History of Dogs*
Prof. Eldwood's *Dogs in Art*
Prof. Eldwood's *Why Dogs Have Hair*
Prof. Eldwood's *Dogs Who Look Like People*
Prof. Eldwood's *Dogs That Don't Shed*
Prof. Eldwood's *Dogs That Do Shed*
Prof. Eldwood's *Relations Between Dogs and Cats*
Prof. Eldwood's *Why Dogs Don't Marry*
Prof. Eldwood's *Geometry Books that Mention Dogs*

He should have a book like Prof. Eldwood's *Care and Feeding of Dogs.*

Fred said, "Isn't this wonderful!"
Kingie didn't say a word.
Fred took the $300 out of his pocket and gave it back to Kingie, thanking him for the loan.

Your Turn to Play

1. Name the largest cardinal number less than ten.
2. What is the smallest ordinal number?
3. How many dogs does Betty have right now?
4. What is the total number of dogs that Alexander and Betty have right now?
5. What number doubled gives you 18?

. . . . **ANSWERS** . . . .

1. The largest cardinal number less than ten is 9.

2. The smallest ordinal number is first.

3. Betty got 15 dogs from the animal shelter. She gave one to Fred.

$$\begin{array}{r} 15 \\ -\ 1 \\ \hline 14 \end{array}$$

4. What is the total number of dogs that Alexander and Betty have right now?

There are two ways you could find the answer.

One way: Add up Alexander's 15 dogs and Betty's 14 dogs.

$$\begin{array}{r} 15 \\ +\ 14 \\ \hline 29 \end{array}$$

Second way: They had 30 dogs and one was given to Fred.

$$\begin{array}{r} 30 \\ -\ 1 \\ \hline 29 \end{array}$$

5. When you double 9 you get 18.

A Row of Practice

52	15	30	7	4	65
+ 17	− 7	+ 8	+ 7	+ 9	+ 85
69	8	38	14	13	150

Chapter Eighteen
One Becomes 30

Fred didn't know how to play with Ralph. Ralph didn't want to play chess. She didn't want to sit down and read a book with Fred. She didn't want to play pretend tea party.

Fred took out a sheet of paper. He knew that everyone liked to draw pictures. He told Ralph, "I'll draw a picture of you, and you draw a picture of me."

Ralph's picture of Fred
and
Fred's picture of Ralph

Fred was so happy. He had found something that he and his dog could do together.

There was a knock on the door. Fred told Ralph, "Stay!" and headed to the door. Ralph followed Fred.*

It was Betty. "We have to talk," she began. "The lease I signed for my apartment says that I'm not allowed to have pets."

Fred said, "What about Alexander's lease?" She shook her head.

---

* Fred didn't know that you have to teach a dog what *stay, sit,* or *rollover* means. Dogs (and babies) do not start out life knowing English.

"Did you check with Joe and Darlene? Do either of their apartments allow dogs?" Fred asked.

She shook her head again.

Kingie knew what was about to happen. He put down his paint brush and put away his easel. He went back and hid in the fort that he had built when Fred had a cat.

Please Fred! Don't say, "Yes."

Fred said, "Yes." Alexander, who was downstairs with 29 dogs, walked up the two flights of stairs, down the hallway with nine vending machines (four on one side and five on the other), and into Fred's office.

Thirty dogs, Betty and Alexander, Fred and Kingie—it was a tight squeeze to fit them all into Fred's office.

$$
\begin{array}{rl}
30 & \text{dogs} \\
2 & \text{B \& A} \\
+\ 2 & \text{F \& K} \\
\hline
34 &
\end{array}
$$

Betty and Alexander thanked Fred. Alexander shook Fred's hand and said, "You're a good man." Betty kissed Fred on the cheek.

Then they left, feeling very relieved that they had found a home for all those dogs.

$$
\begin{array}{rl}
34 & \text{in Fred's office} \\
-\ \ 2 & \text{B \& A leave} \\
\hline
32 & \text{left in Fred's office}
\end{array}
$$

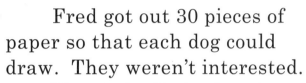

Fred got out 30 pieces of paper so that each dog could draw. They weren't interested.

He tried a little chemistry lecture, but none of them were interested in the different isotopes of hydrogen.*

But the dogs were interested in barking . . . and barking . . . and barking. Thirty dogs in one small room were loud. The other teachers in the building knocked on Fred's door to complain, but Fred couldn't hear them knocking.

Kingie threw a message out of his fort.

---

* All hydrogen atoms have one proton. The different isotopes of hydrogen have different numbers of neutrons.

P	PN	PNN
one isotope	a second isotope	a third isotope

When Fred opened up the paper airplane, the message read: Fred!!! You must walk your stupid dogs!!! Otherwise, there is going to be a big mess in here!!! (Dolls use a lot of exclamation points when they are excited. Good writers use them sparingly.)

Fred had no idea what Kingie meant by "big mess." Then he smelled something. He learned.

He couldn't take all 30 dogs outside at once. He put a leash on one of them and walked him down the hallway (4 + 5 = 9 vending machines), down two flights of stairs, and outside. After the dog was "finished," they walked up the two flights of stairs, down the hallway, and back to the office.

He put a leash on another one of them and walked him down the hallway (4 + 5 = 9 vending machines), down two flights of stairs, and outside. After the dog was "finished," they walked up the two flights of stairs, down the hallway, and back to the office.

He put a leash on another one of them and walked him down the hallway (4 + 5 = 9 vending machines), down two flights of stairs, and outside. After the dog was "finished," they walked up the two flights of stairs, down the hallway, and back to the office.

He put a leash on another one of them and walked him down the hallway (4 + 5 = 9 vending machines), down two flights of stairs, and outside. After the dog was "finished," they walked up the two flights of stairs, down the hallway, and back to the office.

He put a leash on another one of them and walked him down the hallway (4 + 5 = 9 vending machines), down two flights of stairs, and outside. After the dog was "finished," they walked up the two flights of stairs, down the hallway, and back to the office.

He put a leash on another one of them and walked him down the hallway (4 + 5 = 9 vending machines), down two flights of stairs, and outside. After the dog was "finished," they walked up the two flights of stairs, down the hallway, and back to the office.

He put a leash on another one of them and walked him down the hallway (4 + 5 = 9 vending machines), down two flights of stairs, and outside. After the dog was "finished," they walked up the two flights of stairs, down the hallway, and back to the office.

Fred had walked eight of the dogs. Dogs were getting to be a lot less fun for Fred.

He put a leash on another one of them and walked him down the hallway (4 + 5 = 9 vending machines), down two flights of stairs, and outside. After the dog was "finished," they walked up the two flights of stairs, down the hallway, and back to the office.

He put a leash on another one of them and walked him down the hallway (4 + 5 = 9 vending machines), down two flights of stairs, and outside. After the dog was "finished," they walked up the two flights of stairs, down the hallway, and back to the office.

He put a leash on another one of them and walked him down the hallway (4 + 5 = 9 vending machines), down two flights of stairs, and outside. After the dog was "finished," they walked up the two flights of stairs, down the hallway, and back to the office.

He put a leash on another one of them and walked him down the hallway (4 + 5 = 9 vending machines), down two flights of stairs, and outside. After the dog was "finished," they walked up the two flights of stairs, down the hallway, and back to the office.

He put a leash on another one of them and walked him down the hallway (4 + 5 = 9 vending machines), down two flights of stairs, and outside. After the dog was "finished," they walked up the two flights of stairs, down the hallway, and back to the office.

He put a leash on another one of them and walked him down the hallway (4 + 5 = 9 vending machines), down two flights of stairs, and outside. After the dog was "finished," they walked up the two flights of stairs, down the hallway, and back to the office.

He put a leash on another one of them and walked him down the hallway (4 + 5 = 9 vending machines), down two flights of stairs, and outside. After the dog was "finished," they walked up the two flights of stairs, down the hallway, and back to the office.

He put a leash on another one of them and walked him down the hallway (4 + 5 = 9 vending machines), down two flights of stairs, and outside. After the dog was "finished," they walked up the two flights of stairs, down the hallway, and back to the office.

He put a leash on another one of them and walked him down the hallway (4 + 5 = 9 vending machines), down two flights of stairs, and outside. After the dog was "finished," they walked up the two flights of stairs, down the hallway, and back to the office.

He put a leash on another one of them and walked him down the hallway (4 + 5 = 9 vending machines), down two flights of stairs, and outside. After the dog was "finished," they walked up the two flights of stairs, down the hallway, and back to the office.

He put a leash on another one of them and walked him down the hallway (4 + 5 = 9 vending machines), down two flights of stairs, and outside. After the dog was "finished," they walked up the two flights of stairs, down the hallway, and back to the office.

It took 10 minutes to walk a dog. In one hour Fred walked 6 dogs. In 5 hours he had walked all 30 dogs.

 A second message from Kingie informed Fred: *You have to feed your stupid dogs, and I am not going to lend you money!!*

Your Turn to Play

1. If it takes 5 hours to walk all the dogs, and each dog must be walked twice a day, how many hours will Fred spend walking the dogs each day?

2. Other teachers in the building phoned Fred to complain about the barking noise. Fred didn't hear the phone ring because of all the barking.

One of them called the policeman in the billion-dollar Millard Fillmore federally funded campus police station. The policeman went from his office to the exit and then across campus to investigate.

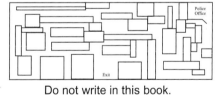

Do not write in this book.

He told Fred that each dog needed a $2 dog license.

Thirty times 2 is the same as 2 times 30 by the

_____ law of multiplication.
<u>Fill in one word</u>

3. Two times 30 means 30 + 30.

30 + 30 = ?

.... ANSWERS ....

1. If Fred has to spend 5 hours twice a day, he will need to spend 5 + 5 hours, which is 10.

2. $30 \times 2 = 2 \times 30$ is an example of the commutative law of multiplication.

    (7 + 5 = 5 + 7 is an example of the commutative law of addition.)

    (Shutting your eyes and going to sleep are not commutative.)

    (Opening your mouth and speaking are not commutative.)

    (Putting money into a vending machine and getting out a can of Sluice are not commutative.)

3. 30 + 30

$$\begin{array}{r} 30 \\ + 30 \\ \hline 60 \end{array}$$

Chapter Nineteen
Dogs

What do you do with a dog? (Other than walk them, feed them, walk them again, take them to the vet for shots, dust them for fleas, and listen to them bark.)

Fred wanted to look on the positive side. Why do some people have a dog?

To play with? Fred got a ball and put a leash on one of the dogs and walked him down the hallway (4 + 5 = 9), down two flights of stairs and outside. He took the leash off, threw the ball and yelled "Fetch." The dog looked at Fred.

After about a half hour, Fred taught his dog the game of fetch. He would throw the ball, and the dog would run and get it and bring it back to Fred.

Fred realized that the only games you could play with a dog are dog games.

Fred would throw the ball, and the dog would bring it back to him. Fred got bored, but the dog would happily play fetch for hours.

Was it for the exercise of throwing the ball? It would be a lot easier just to throw the ball up a hillside and have it roll back down to you.

Fred took the dog back to the office. He threw the ball into the garbage can. It was wet with dog slobber.

To be a life-long companion? Hardly. If a baby and a puppy are born in the same year, the dog will probably be dead when the kid is a teenager. Of course, if you are 85 years old when you buy a dog, it may not die before you do.

To have someone to talk to? Yes. This does work. You can talk *to* a dog. Of course, you can't talk *with* a dog. Fred had been talking to his doll Kingie for years. Kingie was a very good listener. And Kingie didn't shed.

Back at his office, Fred rummaged through his desk drawers and found some half-eaten sandwiches that he had saved. They had been in his desk for weeks. He tossed them to the dogs and they devoured them.

He opened up one of his library books, Prof. Eldwood's *History of Dogs*. He thought that might help him understand why some people have dogs.

Eldwood wrote that dogs are very much like wolves. Wolves like to travel in packs, and they like to follow the head wolf.*

One of the dogs came up and licked Fred's hand. In that instant, Fred realized one big advantage of owning a dog: You get to be the master. They look up to you and will follow you.

❋ Your boss makes you fetch his coffee;
❋ The policeman gives you a ticket;
❋ Your parents make you clean up your
   room;
❋ The clouds rain on you;
❋ A cold puts you in bed; and
❋ Your best friend won't talk to you
   anymore—

but you have a dog. It will lick your hand. It will fetch the ball you throw. It looks up to you. You are the leader. You are the head wolf. (No one has ever figured out how to be a leader for cats.)

If you can't be president or a policeman or a cloud that rains on everybody, at least you can own a dog.

The "problem" with Fred is that he didn't want to be president and rule over other people.

---

* In Eldwood's *History of People* he wrote that people often like to travel in groups and follow the leader. In German, the word for leader is *der Führer*.

He needed love—as everyone does—but he didn't need 30 dogs to give him dog love. He knew that God loved him and that he had friends who loved him.

But he didn't have ten hours each day to walk those dogs. He didn't have money to feed them or get dog licenses.

He phoned everyone he knew and asked them if they would like a dog. No one did.

He took Ralph and the other 29 dogs back to the animal shelter. And he cried.

THE KITTEN Caboodle

The Official Campus Newspaper of KITTENS University   10¢

late breaking news
No Doggies to Die
Saved!

KANSAS: Mrs. Hund, head of the KITTENS Animal Shelter, announced minutes ago that the shelter has received a gift of $50,000 from a wealthy artist.

The money will be used to expand the shelter and provide 10,000 new cages for the dogs and cats.

"No longer will we have crowding problems," Hund told the KITTEN Caboodle. "Every animal can stay here until it is adopted. No more euthanasia."

The donor wished to remain anonymous. All that Hund could say was that the donor was six inches tall and wore a baseball cap with KFF on it.

Index

If you would like to
learn more about
books written about
Fred . . .

FredGauss.com

Gauss is Fred's last name.
It rhymes with house.